POLICY AND PRACTICE IN HEALT
NUMBER TWENTY-TWO

Domestic Abuse

Contemporary Perspectives and Innovative Practices

POLICY AND PRACTICE IN HEALTH AND SOCIAL CARE

See www.dunedinacademicpress.co.uk for details of all our publications

POLICY AND PRACTICE IN HEALTH AND SOCIAL CARE
SERIES EDITORS
CHARLOTTE L. CLARKE AND CHARLOTTE PEARSON

Domestic Abuse
Contemporary Perspectives and Innovative Practices

Edited by

**Oona Brooks-Hay, Michele Burman
and Clare McFeely**

EDINBURGH ◆ LONDON

First published in 2018 by Dunedin Academic Press Ltd.
Head Office: Hudson House, 8 Albany Street, Edinburgh EH1 3QB
London Office: 352 Cromwell Tower, Barbican, London EC2Y 8NB

ISBNs:
9781780460598 (Paperback)
9781780465944 (ePub)
9781780465951 (Kindle)

British Library Cataloguing in Publication Data
A catalogue record for this book is available from the British Library

Typeset by Makar Publishing Production, Edinburgh
Printed in Great Britain by CPI Antony Rowe

CONTENTS

ACKNOWLEDGEMENTS

Editing this book has been a very positive collaborative experience and we are grateful to the many people who supported and encouraged us in this process.

We would like to thank the contributing authors for their hard work and willingness to share their expertise, and Maureen McBride for her support with the manuscript. Also Emma Forbes and Lesley Walker, Barbara Adzajlic and Nel Whiting for their invaluable feedback, which helped to shape Chapters 4 and 6.

Our particular thanks to Charlotte Pearson and Anthony Kinahan for encouraging the development of this book and for their patience. The writing process was prolonged by impending legislative changes and the birth of four babies (Rosa, Lachlan, Stanley and Theo).

Perhaps most importantly, we would like to acknowledge the inspirational and tireless work of the feminist activists who collectively drove forward the work described in this volume and individually taught us much.

GLOSSARY OF ABBREVIATIONS

ASP	Additional Support Plan
ASSIST	Advocacy Support Safety Information Services Together
CfE	Curriculum for Excellence
COPFS	Crown Office and Procurator Fiscal Service
CSA	childhood sexual abuse
DACU	Domestic Abuse Coordination Unit
DALO	domestic abuse liaison officer
DSDAS	Disclosure Scheme for Domestic Abuse in Scotland
DVPP	domestic violence perpetrator programme
GBV	gender-based violence
GIRFEC	*Getting It Right for Every Child*
GLM	Good Lives Model
HMIC	Her Majesty's Inspectorate of Constabulary
IPV	intimate partner violence
IT	intimate terrorism
MARAC	Multi-Agency Risk Assessment Conferences
MATAC	Multi-Agency Tasking and Coordinating
MVP	Mentors in Violence Prevention
NCYPPN	National Children and Young People's Prevention Network
NICE	National Institute for Health and Care Excellence
NSPCC	National Society for the Prevention of Cruelty to Children
ONS	Office for National Statistics
PEACH	preventing domestic abuse for children
RCEM	Royal College of Emergency Medicine
RSHPE	relationships, sexual health and parenthood education
SCCJR	Scottish Centre for Crime and Justice Research
SCJS	Scottish Crime and Justice Survey
SCV	situational couple violence
SGHD	Scottish Government Health Directorate
SLAB	Scottish Legal Aid Board
SWA	Scottish Women's Aid

UK	United Kingdom
UN	United Nations
UNCRC	United Nations Convention on the Rights of the Child
US	United States
VAW	Violence Against Women
VIA	Victim Information and Advice
VR	violent resistance
WHA	World Health Assembly
WHO	World Health Organization

CONTRIBUTOR BIOGRAPHIES

Dr Oona Brooks-Hay is a Lecturer in Criminology at the University of Glasgow. She has worked as a researcher and practitioner in the field of gender-based violence for more than twenty years with a particular interest in domestic abuse and sexual offences. Oona is a coordinator of the Scottish Gender Based Violence Research Network and the founder of the Glasgow University Gender Based Violence Research Forum.

Michele Burman is Professor of Criminology and Head of the School of Social and Political Sciences at the University of Glasgow and a founding co-Director of the Scottish Centre for Crime and Justice Research (SCCJR). She has long-standing research interests in gender, crime and justice, with a particular interest in criminal justice responses to gender-based violence.

Katie Cosgrove is the National Programme Manager for Gender Based Violence and Health in NHS Scotland, with responsibility for leading the work in NHS SCOTLAND to improve the healthcare identification and management of such abuse. She has worked in the field of gender and gender-based violence (GBV) for twenty-six years at both an operational and strategic level. She is a specialist technical advisor to the World Health Organization (WHO) on violence against women, contributing to its gender mainstreaming, GBV and reproductive health programmes.

Roy Harris is an educational practitioner who works with primary school children. He has a particular interest in innovative education practices and is passionate about how critical thought in children can be encouraged.

Dr Nancy Lombard is a Reader in Sociology and Social Policy at Glasgow Caledonian University. She devised gender equality training for educational practitioners. Nancy was a Core Expert with the European Network of Experts on Gender Equality and currently sits on the Scottish government's Strategic Board for the implementation of *Equally Safe*.

Dr Clare McFeely is a Lecturer in Nursing and Health Care at the University of Glasgow. Before moving to education, Clare worked in the NHS initially as a midwife and then in research and development roles, latterly focusing on the health response to survivors of GBV. Clare is also a founder member and coordinator of the Scottish Gender Based Violence Research Network.

Anna Mitchell is the Domestic Abuse Lead Officer in Edinburgh, having worked in a variety of domestic abuse settings and in local and national government operational and strategic roles for more than twenty years. She is interested in how child welfare systems engage with fathers who perpetrate domestic abuse in order to increase the safety of women and children.

Dr Fiona Morrison 'is a lecturer at the Centre for Child Wellbeing and Protection at the University of Stirling. Her research interests are in the areas of children's rights, child welfare, domestic abuse and social work with children and families.

FOREWORD
'IT'S DIFFERENT IN SCOTLAND'

Anyone who has worked in policy or academic collaborations on Violence Against Women (VAW) at the United Kingdom (UK) or international level has said: 'It's different in Scotland.' In 1999, devolution provided an opportunity for Scotland to reconsider VAW policy. Scotland's Women's Aid (SWA) movement wasted no time in lobbying for change, recorded in this iconic image of a march down Princes Street in Edinburgh the same year, while calling for a new law addressing domestic abuse.

Twenty years later, in 2019, the recently passed Domestic Abuse (Scotland) Act 2018 will commence, and Scotland will operationalise a law founded on the feminist theory, research and practice outlined so ably by the authors of this book. The vote on the Bill was followed by a standing ovation by Members of the Scottish Parliament (MSPs) for domestic abuse survivors and campaigners watching from the public gallery. It's different in Scotland, indeed.

The passage of the new Act, and the year's pause before it commences, offer immense challenges and opportunities for Scotland's intention to eradicate domestic abuse. This book could not be more timely as it presents the challenges encountered during the evolution of policy and practice in Scotland and explores some critical issues that remain. Measuring domestic abuse via police reports and survey data has never provided satisfactory results. Given the newly expanded definition (see Chapter 2), this strategy will prove even less helpful. What is required is a strategic commitment to improved analysis on the part of the Scottish government.

The problem of dual arrests and the overarching issue of inappropriate arrest and charging of victims for domestic abuse are matters of grave concern for SWA. Arrests of women as 'perpetrators' of violence against male partners and ex-partners have steadily risen and then levelled off in the last ten years, as discussed in Chapter 3. The impact of these arrests on women, especially women with children, is massive and harmful, and the risk of a similar trend when the new law is implemented is worrying. We have always considered this a signal for improved police training and supervision.

Understanding children's experiences as victims and holding the abuser responsible rather than the non-offending parent (read, mother) requires a seismic shift in child protection and welfare systems in Scotland. Practice that frames children's experience of abuse as what David Mandel calls 'a parenting choice' made by abusive parents is one of Scotland's massive challenges in the decade ahead, and Chapter 7 describes early and important work in Edinburgh to implement system change through adoption of Safe and Together practice principles.

Until recently, children's experiences were largely considered when they were 'direct' victims of abuse or in narrowly focused 'prevention' work that focused on calls for schools to teach (or, more often, ask local Women's Aid groups to teach) teenagers that violence is bad (as if 'violence' is a homogenous phenomenon and with little or no challenge to institutional and systemic sexism). What a breath of fresh air then is the discussion in Chapter 6 of how the education sector can do primary prevention, by challenging gendered stereotypes in the classroom and curriculum.

The new policy and legislation in Scotland cannot and will not improve the lives of those living with domestic abuse if the services that support them gradually disappear as the new law is implemented. Much good practice has been developed, in health as well as in local support services in Scotland (Chapters 5 and 7). This progress is in significant jeopardy unless strategic leadership emerges in government directorates other than equalities and justice and in local authorities (see Chapter 8).

Finally, it is worth noting that this book is written by both academics and practitioners. It reflects decades of collaborative research, policy influencing and advocacy. Working to transform research and practice, the authors have produced a body of work that frames and supports social change and the sometimes halting progress towards justice for those experiencing domestic abuse. These collaborations bode well for Scotland, and long may they continue.

Dr Marsha Scott, Scottish Women's Aid

CHAPTER 1

Introducing Scotland's Approach to Domestic Abuse

Oona Brooks-Hay, Michele Burman and Clare McFeely

Introduction

Domestic abuse is a persistent and globally pervasive health and social problem that cuts across the boundaries of age, class, ethnicity and sexual orientation (McCue, 2008). It is estimated that one in four women will experience domestic abuse in their lifetime (Council of Europe, 2002; FRA, 2014), affecting 'vastly greater numbers of people than global terrorism' (Pain, 2012, p. 6). The effects of domestic abuse at both an individual and societal level are long-term and far-reaching – extending well beyond the experiences of individual women and children to the wider community. Hence, addressing domestic abuse is (or should be) a pressing concern for academics and practitioners working across a broad range of sectors including health, education, housing, social work, criminal justice, law and politics, especially as substantial challenges remain in terms of how to define, conceptualise, prevent and respond to this abuse.

At an international level, significant progress has been made in addressing domestic abuse and developments in this field have evolved rapidly in recent years. Even within the context of these improvements, Scotland is recognised as a leader in work to combat domestic abuse specifically, and VAW more broadly (Charles and Mackay, 2013; Coy *et al.*, 2007; Lombard and Whiting, 2015; Stark, 2007). Most recently, the Domestic Abuse (Scotland) Act 2018 has been described by Professor Evan Stark as setting 'a new gold standard' (Brooks, 2018). By drawing upon research evidence and innovative practices emanating from Scotland, and setting them within an international context, this book aims to make a timely contribution to understanding and informing contemporary responses to domestic abuse by articulating the unique approach adopted in Scotland.

Underpinning feminist and human rights commitments

Scotland is a relatively small country with a population of just over five million people. Yet its devolved status, consultative approach to policy development and implementation, active feminist movement and the consequent definition of domestic abuse as an inequalities issue render it particularly interesting both politically and academically.

Scotland's approach to tackling domestic abuse is underpinned by international treaties and human rights obligations shared by other countries. They include the:

- Council of Europe Convention on Preventing and Combating Violence against Women and Domestic Violence (2011) (the Istanbul Convention);
- Global Platform for Action (1995) calling on governments to take integrated measures to prevent and eliminate violence against women and girls;
- Human Rights Act (1988), which incorporates the protections set out in the European Convention on Human Rights into Scots law;
- United Nations Convention on the Elimination of Discrimination Against Women (CEDAW) (1979), an agenda for action to end all forms of discrimination against women;
- United Nations Convention on the Rights of the Child (UNCRC), an international human rights treaty that grants all children and young people aged seventeen and under a comprehensive set of rights (Scottish Government, 2016a).

Though the 'Istanbul Convention' has yet to be ratified by the UK government, the Scottish government outlined its commitment to meeting the moral and legal obligations set out by these treaties as a 'modern democratic Country' in *Equally Safe* (Scottish Government, 2016a), its strategy for the prevention and eradication of violence against women and girls. This strategy aspires to:

> the creation of an inclusive Scotland which protects, respects and realises the human rights of everyone. And whilst we are focusing on preventing and eradicating violence against women

and girls in Scotland, we cannot forget that all over the world women and girls are experiencing abuse and violence every hour of every day (Scottish Government, 2016a, pp. 21–2).

Scotland has a strong history of feminist activism in relation to VAW, which has effectively engaged in policymaking processes and helped to shape the Scottish approach to domestic abuse (Charles and Mackay, 2013; Hearn and McKie, 2010). Refuges for women fleeing domestic abuse opened in Scotland in 1973 in Edinburgh and Glasgow, and by 1976 Scottish Women's Aid (SWA), a national third-sector refuge organisation, was formed (Cuthbert and Irving, 2001). Evidence to support this work began to emerge through feminist academics, most notably from pioneering research conducted in Scotland by Dobash and Dobash (1979). In the following decades, feminist activists in Scotland lobbied for the acknowledgement of domestic abuse as a social problem that required state action and resources. They deployed tenacious and creative strategies, exemplified by the radical Zero Tolerance campaign of the early 1990s, to effect social change by challenging gendered power relations and addressing misconceptions about domestic abuse and other related forms of violence against women and children (Mackay, 1996).

The changing political landscape of the UK in the 1990s provided further opportunities to enhance the Scottish response to domestic abuse. In 1999, political control of areas most pertinent to addressing domestic abuse were devolved to the new Scottish Parliament, namely: education, health, housing, civil and criminal law, policing and local government (Charles and Mackay, 2013, p. 606). Since its inception, the Scottish Parliament has developed a distinctive approach to policy development and implementation that enables consideration of political, social and cultural factors (Cairney *et al.*, 2016). A key characteristic of the Scottish approach is government consultation with stakeholders from the private, public and third (voluntary) sector to develop policy, thus enabling voices such as the feminist movement to be heard. The women's sector successfully mobilised to achieve what Mackay (2010) terms 'feminist constitutional activism' in the devolution process. This saw: the adoption of equal opportunities as one of the key principles of the new Scottish Parliament; the creation of equality policy machinery in government and an equal-opportunities committee; a commitment to gender equality mainstreaming; and the greater participation of women's organisations in a more inclusive style of policymaking (Burman and Johnstone, 2015).

A national strategy and infrastructure

Immediately following devolution, fundamental building blocks that would provide an infrastructure for future responses to domestic abuse were put in place. In 2000, the first national strategy to address domestic abuse was launched. Developed by the multi-sectoral Scottish Partnership on Domestic Abuse, a national action plan set domestic abuse as a national priority with an approach known as the three 'Ps': *prevention* of risk of violence; *protection* of victims and potential victims; and *provision* of services to deal with the consequences of domestic abuse (Scottish Executive, 2001). This later extended to four 'Ps', with the addition of *participation* to promote inclusion of those exposed to domestic abuse. Soon after, the National Domestic Abuse Helpline and the Domestic Abuse Service Development Fund were launched and a Scottish government VAW team was created to ensure a consistent approach across government (then the Scottish Executive) (Charles and Mackay, 2013).

In reviewing levels of service provision across the UK, Coy *et al.* (2007, p. 5) state that:

> The best story is to be told in Scotland [...] The reason is simple; the Scottish government is developing a strategic approach to addressing violence against women and has allocated ring-fenced funding for services.

Therefore, at a national level, devolution has enabled the growth of a positive underpinning and provision of considerable resources to address the consequences of VAW. Provision has since developed with the allocation of two key funds: the national VAW fund and a separate Rape Crisis Specific fund, the creation of which recognised the need for dedicated investment in this field and reduced competition for specialist third-sector organisations for funds from more generic sources. This commitment to funding has been lauded internationally; however, in Scotland there is concern that the funds available are still insufficient to adequately meet the demands upon service providers. SWA, the main specialist provider of support and refuge for those experiencing domestic abuse, report that almost half (46%) of women and their children who request refuge are turned away due to a lack of safe and suitable spaces (SWA, 2016a). Moreover, the 'Scottish Women's Aid survey of funding for Women's Aid services 2016' revealed that two in five of its thirty-six local groups had to make cuts to their services because of reduced funding at a time when 52% of groups reported an increase in demand for their services (SWA, 2016b).

Devolution has also resulted in a complicated architecture of multi-level government that differs from the rest of the UK. This multi-level approach supports local adaptation of national policy and has devolved aspects of resource allocation to the thirty-two local authorities within Scotland, thus enabling allocation with consideration of local priorities (e.g. rurality). The combination of local decision-making and a consultative approach can result in different levels of attention, as well as associated development, review and investment, over time for some policy issues (Cairney et al., 2016). Indeed, a recent review of specialist domestic abuse service provision found limited accessibility of support in some areas and called for parity of provision across regions in Scotland and an end to 'postcode lottery' for those affected by domestic abuse (SafeLives, 2017).

A gendered analysis

Most significantly, in 2000 the Scottish government adopted a gendered definition of domestic abuse. This gendered analysis echoes the United Nations (UN) Declaration on the Elimination of Violence Against Women (1993) and explicitly positions domestic abuse as both a cause and consequence of gender inequality whereby women are disproportionately affected (McFeely et al., 2013). This gendered approach is more radical than that adopted in other parts of the UK, whereby a gender-neutral and ostensibly criminal justice framing has been adopted (Charles and Mackay, 2013). In addition, the adoption of the term 'domestic abuse', rather than 'domestic violence', better represents the combination of psychological and physical dimensions of violence to broaden the focus from physical abuse to the ongoing manipulation of power in intimate relationships (Scottish Executive, 2000; 2003). In a UK-wide review of service provision for VAW, the Scottish approach was held up as an example of good practice:

Scotland should [...] be regarded as a benchmark with respect to its strategic approach, its recognition that violence is a cause and consequence of women's inequality and its commitment to enhancing capacity and diversity of provision. National and regional governments should follow the model of the Scottish Government in developing VAW strategies which have a core commitment to funding specialised support services (Coy *et al.*, 2007, p. 7).

The Scottish government's most recent strategy, *Equally Safe* (Scottish Government, 2014a, updated in Scottish Government, 2016a) ultimately aims to eradicate violence against women and girls in Scotland, by addressing persistent inequalities between women and men, including the gender pay gap, occupational segregation, disproportionate levels of economic dependence, and institutional sexism. The approach adopted remains consistent in relation to the four 'Ps' but more explicitly places domestic abuse within the wider context of violence against women and gender inequality. Hence, ensuring that women and girls 'thrive as equal citizens: socially, culturally, economically and politically' is a key priority within the strategy. The gendered analysis adopted within *Equally Safe* acknowledges that men are also victims of violence and abuse, though women and girls are disproportionately affected by particular forms of violence due to their gender and the status they are accorded within society. Importantly, *Equally Safe* acknowledges men's crucial role in challenging gendered norms and inequalities.

Embedding a gendered analysis of domestic abuse in policy and service provision marks significant progress in this area, but there is a recognition of current limitations in addressing the intersections of domestic abuse and issues such as age, ethnicity, sexual orientation, socio-economic and health status. The Scottish response is developing in these areas: for example, through provision of services exclusively for women from Black and minority ethnic groups; and by the development of a national policy on tackling forced marriage (Chantler *et al.*, 2017). However, the evidence base regarding these intersections is underdeveloped and the authors acknowledge that this is reflected in the content of this book.

The content and approach adopted by this book

A feminist theoretical perspective, which recognises domestic abuse as a function of gendered inequalities, will be outlined and adopted as a framework for understanding the research evidence and practices discussed throughout the book. This is a perspective shared by the contributing authors and it is reflected in the approach adopted by the Scottish government. While this book focuses on domestic abuse as a specific form of GBV, it is acknowledged that domestic abuse constitutes a part of a continuum of male VAW (Kelly, 1988), which impacts upon the daily lives of women and girls irrespective of their personal experiences of violence:

> A great deal of the literature on male violence discusses the areas of male violence separately, such as domestic violence, rape and sexual assault, child sexual abuse, pornography and sexual harassment. But women experience all of these forms of violence. If they do not actually experience the abuse personally, fear exists as a result of other women's experiences. This has a controlling effect on a woman, curtailing their freedom, adding undue stress to their lives, and affecting their confidence (Jannette de Haan, Co-ordinator of Women's Support Project 1992–2012, cited in Scottish Government, 2016a, p. 26).

With regard to the terminology adopted in this book, the term 'domestic abuse' is used to reflect the Scottish context, although it is acknowledged that the terms 'domestic violence' or 'intimate partner violence' (IPV) are cited more widely in other countries. Definitional issues have important implications for the ways that domestic abuse is understood and measured; this will be addressed in Chapter 2.

Similarly, terms used to describe those who experience domestic abuse have been the subject of some discussion. Despite the experience of domestic abuse being one of victimisation, describing those exposed to it as 'victims' can imply passivity (Groves and Thomas, 2014). The term 'victim' is, therefore, often replaced with the term 'survivor' or 'victim–survivor' in recognition of the strengths, rather than the vulnerabilities, of those exposed to abuse (Bewley and Welch, 2014). The term 'survivor' has been commonly adopted in Scotland alongside the longer nomenclature of those who have experienced or have been exposed to domestic abuse. However, the term 'victim' is also commonly used when referring to civil and criminal justice processes. The terms that appear in this book reflect the range of disciplines that have contributed.

Conclusion

In this chapter, we have presented an overview of the unique Scottish approach to domestic abuse and highlighted contemporary issues: domestic abuse is a multifaceted problem with diverse consequences and challenges. Scottish policy has developed consistently over the past twenty years, with cognisance of both wider global direction and local needs, to locate actions to address this abuse within an inequalities framework. Despite considerable strategic investment, however, domestic abuse remains an intractable issue in Scotland.

The following chapters will continue to explore the effectiveness of the current approach and the challenges encountered in a range of settings. This includes discipline-specific challenges and innovations from policing, criminal justice, health, education and social work, as well as broader challenges associated with delivering a collaborative response that meets the needs of survivors and which ultimately aims to eradicate domestic abuse. This book has been designed so that each chapter can be read independently; however, to provide clarity and avoid duplication in this short volume, the following chapter discusses the conceptual underpinning of subsequent chapters. In Chapter 2, Brooks-Hay and Burman also explore the nature and extent of domestic abuse in Scotland and the thorny issues relating to its definition and measurement. Chapter 3 by Brooks-Hay then focuses on the policing of domestic abuse, including innovations in practice and the challenges of addressing domestic abuse as a complex and gendered pattern of behaviour within a law-enforcement context. Continuing the focus on the domestic abuse as a crime, in Chapter 4, Burman charts significant reforms within the criminal justice system and reflects upon the implications of introducing a new statutory offence of domestic abuse in Scotland. In Chapter 5, McFeely and Cosgrove consider domestic abuse as a global public health problem and give an account of the Scottish system-wide response to this issue, including the responsibility of health professionals to ask about abuse. The role of preventative education within primary and secondary schools is discussed by Lombard and Harris in Chapter 6, where it is argued that early intervention and a 'whole school approach', underpinned by an appreciation of gendered (in)equalities, is key to preventing domestic abuse. Retaining a focus on children, in Chapter 7, Morrison and Mitchell highlight the important role of children and families' social work in addressing the adverse impact of domestic abuse on children who are affected by it. They conclude by considering the potential of the innovative 'Safe and Together Model' to transform how social workers respond to children, adult victims and perpetrators of domestic abuse. In the final chapter, McFeely, Burman and Brooks-Hay return to the book's underpinning focus on conceptualising, responding to and preventing domestic abuse as they reflect on persistent and newly emerging challenges alongside innovations in policy, practice and research.

CHAPTER 2

Understanding, Defining and Measuring Domestic Abuse

Oona Brooks-Hay and Michele Burman

Introduction

Naming and defining domestic abuse is by no means a politically neutral process (Groves and Thomas, 2014). The outcome of this process varies between countries, and the institutions within them, according to a range of ideological and pragmatic concerns. Yet the way in which domestic abuse is defined has significant implications for how it is understood, measured and responded to. In turn, how we measure domestic abuse impacts upon how (and whether) we 'see' its complex nature and full extent. This chapter highlights differing approaches to defining domestic abuse and reviews what is known about the nature and extent of the problem by drawing upon data from Scotland and elsewhere. Key areas of contention within the data sources are discussed: namely, the extent to which domestic abuse is gendered and the context that it occurs within. It is argued that the adoption of an empirically and theoretically informed analysis is required to move beyond simplistic incident-based approaches to understanding and measuring domestic abuse.

The Scottish approach to understanding and defining domestic abuse

Domestic abuse is an issue that cuts across international borders though a variety of terms are used within different countries, and these terms have changed over time as theoretical and empirical understandings of domestic abuse have evolved. Early accounts of domestic abuse described 'wife battery', 'wife abuse' and 'wife assault' (Browning and

Dutton, 1986; Dobash and Dobash, 1979; Ford, 1983). More recently, the terms 'domestic violence', 'domestic abuse', 'intimate partner violence', 'intimate terrorism' and 'coercive control' have gained currency. The term adopted reflects the temporal, political and cultural space in which it is used. In the UK, there is no single agreed definition of domestic abuse. There is a long-standing preference in Scotland for use of the term 'domestic abuse' since it reflects the fact that physical violence is only one aspect of what constitutes this abuse. In England and Wales, the Home Office has recently moved from using the term 'domestic violence' to the broader term 'domestic violence and abuse' (Home Office, 2013).

The most recent definitional change witnessed in Scotland, as will be discussed within this chapter, is the adoption of a new 'bespoke' statutory criminal offence of domestic abuse under the Domestic Abuse (Scotland) Act 2018. For the purpose of measuring and understanding domestic abuse, it is important to note that the legal definition of domestic abuse does not necessarily mirror that favoured by government policy documents – this is the case in Scotland and in other jurisdictions.

The Scottish Government's definition

Scotland's approach to understanding and defining VAW is based upon the UN Declaration on the Elimination of Violence Against Women and, as discussed in Chapter 1, it has gained international recognition because of the gendered analysis that underpins this approach. Since 2000, the Scottish government has adopted the following gendered definition of domestic abuse, as identified in its first national strategy to address the issue:

> Domestic Abuse, as gendered based violence, can be perpetrated by partners or ex partners and can include physical abuse (assault and physical attack involving a range of behaviour), sexual abuse (acts which degrade and humiliate women and are perpetrated against their will, including rape) and mental and emotional abuse (such as threats, verbal abuse, racial abuse, withholding money and other types of controlling behaviour such as isolation from family and friends).

The Scottish government (2016a, p. 13) emphasises that its gendered analysis:

firmly places the different forms of violence against women within the gendered reality of men's and women's lives, what it means to be a man and a woman in our society and the status and privileges which are afforded to us depending on whether we are born a man or a woman.

A gendered approach entails recognising the social construction of masculinity, femininity and gender relations within wider structures of gender inequality. From a feminist perspective, it has been argued that domestic abuse is predominately perpetrated by men against women as a display of power and control; as such, it is not gender-neutral (Dobash and Dobash, 2004). Therefore, a gendered analysis of domestic abuse necessitates an understanding of who does what to whom (Hester, 2013) and is also grounded in an appreciation of the context in which this abuse happens, including societal expectations of how men and women should behave. While it has been argued that the occurrence of domestic abuse within same-sex relationships demonstrates that abusive behaviour is a power issue rather than a gender issue (Elliot, 1996), Whiting (2007) eloquently argues that a gendered analysis remains relevant to the experiences of lesbian, gay, bisexual, transgendered, intersex and queer individuals when considered in the broader context of patriarchy. If domestic abuse is not recognised as gendered, the context in which it occurs is lost (Nichols, 2013). Arguably, opportunities to prevent and eradicate it are, therefore, also lost.

In addition to the gendered analysis underpinning the Scottish government's definition of domestic abuse, this definition is noteworthy due to its focus specifically on abuse between partners and ex-partners, rather than between family members. This approach has not been replicated in other parts of the UK; in England and Wales, the Westminster government defines domestic violence and abuse as occurring between those 'who are or have been intimate partners or family members'. This conflation between family violence and intimate partner violence has been critiqued on the basis that it wrongly assumes that the dynamics of family violence (e.g. between siblings or parents and children) are the same as the dynamic of intimate partner violence (Kelly and Westmarland, 2016). However, it has also been argued that focusing exclusively on the relationship between a partner or ex-partner can be problematic as other family members – male and female – may contribute to or exacerbate domestic abuse in ethnic minority families (Mirza, 2016). There are clear implications here for measuring domestic abuse; an issue common to all forms of domestic abuse data collection is that domestic abuse comprises a range of different behaviours only identifiable as such because of the relationship between the victim and the perpetrator (Walby *et al.*, 2017).

The Scottish legal definition of domestic abuse

Following the passage of the Domestic Abuse (Scotland) Act 2018, a specific criminal offence of domestic abuse has been created in Scotland for the first time. Previously, no statutory criminal offence or definition of domestic abuse existed. A key feature of the new offence lies in its incorporation, within a single offence, of a wide range of behaviour that may constitute domestic abuse including emotional and psychological abuse. In some other jurisdictions (including England and Wales), a less radical approach has been adopted; coercive and controlling behaviour has been criminalised and added to the suite of existing offences that domestic abuse can be prosecuted under, but a specific offence of domestic abuse has not been created.

The new Scottish offence draws upon the concept of 'coercive control' (Stark, 2007) though it stops short of using this term because of the complexities of defining this conduct in criminal code. Stark's (2007) depiction of 'coercive control' brings to the fore everyday strategies abusive men use to entrap women in their personal life over time, without necessarily enacting physical violence to exert control. By conceptualising domestic abuse as coercive control, Stark frames this phenomenon as an ongoing course of conduct rather than an incident, or even a series of incidents, and the severity of abuse is determined by its consequences in terms of control over an individual rather than the violent or non-violent acts used to perpetrate coercive control per se. Within the scope of the new offence, 'abusive behaviour' is understood to be that which is 'violent, threatening or intimidating' and would be considered by a 'reasonable person' likely to have the effect of: making a partner or ex-partner dependent on or subordinate to the perpetrator; isolating them from friends, relatives or other sources of support; controlling, regulating or monitoring their day-to-day activities; depriving or restricting their freedom of action; or frightening, humiliating, degrading or punishing them.

Importantly, the new offence also stipulates that for an offence of domestic abuse to have been committed the behaviour needs to have occurred on at least two occasions (demonstrating a 'course of behaviour'), recognising that domestic abuse is characterised by an ongoing pattern of conduct. This is a significant attempt to move away from the problematic 'incident-based' approach to policing and prosecuting domestic abuse. The implications of the new offence for the policing and prosecution of domestic abuse will be discussed in more detail in Chapters 3 and 4. For the purposes of the current discussion, however, it is noteworthy that the legal definition of domestic abuse adopted in any jurisdiction will have significant implications for the way in which it is understood and measured by administrative data such as police statistics, not least in terms of the behaviour that it incorporates, the relationships within which it occurs, and the gender of victims and perpetrators. For clarity, the offence of domestic abuse in Scotland is gender-neutral, contrary to the Scottish government's gendered definition.

Measuring the nature and extent of the problem

Key data sources on domestic abuse in Scotland and elsewhere include police statistics, crime surveys, data gathered by support agencies and empirical research studies. Arguably, each of these data sources has limitations, but taken as a whole they illuminate different aspects of the problem and assist in identifying changing trends over time. Relevant data from these sources is reviewed below, providing an overview of the nature and extent of domestic abuse in Scotland while highlighting key issues to consider when viewing domestic abuse data more broadly.

Scottish police data

Incidents of domestic abuse reported to the police provide an important insight into domestic abuse cases entering the criminal justice system. The Domestic Abuse Recorded by the Police in Scotland annual statistical bulletin forms part of a series of bulletins produced by the Scottish government on the criminal justice system. As such, this bulletin provides a useful point of comparison over time, and it includes data on the number of incidents reported, where and when these incidents took place, and the age and gender of victims and alleged perpetrators. In 2016/17, there were 58,810 incidents of domestic abuse recorded by the police in Scotland; this equated to 109 recorded incidents per 10,000 population. Although this represents only a 1% increase from the previous year, the number of domestic abuse incidents recorded by the police has risen markedly over the past ten years. Since 2005/06 these incidents have increased from 45,331 per year, but have remained relatively stable at around 60,000 annually since 2011/12.

The rise in incidents recorded by the police over time is unlikely to be the result of an actual increase in domestic abuse; it is more likely to be indicative of changes in police practice, enhanced awareness of domestic abuse and improved victim confidence in the police response, culminating in a growing number of reports. Yet, domestic abuse still remains a notoriously under-reported crime. Under-reporting is by no means unique to domestic abuse though the sensitive and complex nature of domestic abuse means that it remains one of the most under-reported crimes (MacQueen and Norris, 2014). Many victims do not self-classify their experiences as domestic abuse or as a crime (Groves and Thomas, 2014), and even those who do may not want to invoke a criminal justice response to their situation. This issue is particularly pertinent to domestic abuse as a crime nested within intimate relationships.

While police data may only ever provide a partial account of the extent of domestic abuse (Walby *et al.*, 2017), it does give us a helpful indication of the police response. In 2016/17, for example, less than half (47%) of incidents reported to the police resulted in an offence being recorded, indicating a high level of attrition at the early stage of the criminal justice process.

The Scottish Crime and Justice Survey (SCJS)

As large-scale surveys of individuals within households, national crime surveys fulfil a useful role in illuminating the 'dark figure of crime' – that is, the extent of crimes that do not come to the attention of the police. Findings from the SCJS consistently indicate that only around one in five incidents of domestic abuse are reported to the police. For this reason, the SCJS and other national crime surveys are particularly relevant to understanding the extent of domestic abuse. The SCJS includes a specific self-completion module on partner abuse and provides an indicator of national prevalence, albeit with some notable limitations.

Headline findings from the SCJS 2014/15 (Scottish Government, 2016d) indicate that 3.4% of women and 2.4% of men had experienced partner abuse in the past year, while 18.5% of women and 9.2% of men had experienced partner abuse since the age of sixteen. The group at the highest risk of partner abuse (in the past twelve months) was young women between the ages of 16–24. With regard to the nature of abuse experienced, on average two different types of physical abuse and three types of psychological abuse were experienced. The most prevalent types of physical abuse were being kicked or bitten (5.2%), pushed or held down (5%) or having something thrown at you with the intention of causing harm (4.7%). Meanwhile, the most common forms of psychological abuse reported were jealous or controlling behaviour (7.6%) and repeatedly being put down by a partner (6.4%).

In viewing the findings from crime surveys, particular attention must be paid to the definition and approach adopted, and the subsequent impact this has on findings. In keeping with other crime surveys, the SCJS refers to incidents yet domestic abuse is characterised by its ongoing and repeated nature. Drawing upon the work of Hearn (1998), Kelly and Westmarland (2016, p. 125) contend that the 'incidentalising' approach adopted in crime surveys reflects the way that violent men account for their behaviour, rather than the experiences of survivors and fails to capture the 'heart and reality' of domestic abuse as a course of conduct. More fundamentally, attempting to capture data about domestic abuse in a crime survey is particularly challenging given that much of the controlling behaviour that constitutes domestic abuse (e.g. a particular look or restricting clothing choices) does not, on its own, equate to a criminal act.

Myhill (2017) critiques the focus on 'acts' within surveys at the expense of impacts of abuse, noting that this approach has led to estimates of male and female perpetration of domestic abuse being similar (as reported in the SCJS), despite this being a picture that does not reflect the findings or experience of specialist researchers or front-line practitioners working in this field. A further limitation of the SCJS, particularly in relation to domestic abuse, lies with the use of residential addresses as part of the sampling method for identifying respondents. This means that women living in refuges, a group who are likely to be among those most seriously affected by domestic abuse and able to identify their experiences as domestic abuse, are excluded by this survey. Conducting a survey within private households where family may be present also has obvious limitations.

MacQueen (2016), however, defends the SCJS arguing that its findings are too readily dismissed due to its most publicised and misleading finding that men and women are at a similar risk of abuse. She goes on to suggest that more detailed analysis of the SCJS has the potential to illuminate experiences of abuse in more meaningful ways, particularly in terms of how risk factors such as age, sexual orientation, disability, religious affiliation and social deprivation intersect with gender. More nuanced analysis and interpretation of SCJS findings, particularly in relation to intersectionalities, would be beneficial and may go some way to addressing the survey's limitations.

Insights from dedicated empirical research and survey data
The nature and extent of domestic abuse

Notwithstanding the challenges of establishing the nature and extent of domestic abuse, survey methodologies and research findings have evolved considerably at a national and international level in recent decades. Dedicated domestic abuse surveys have gone some way to overcoming problems associated with low rates of disclose found in more conventional victimisation surveys (Myhill, 2017). However, there is currently no dedicated national prevalence study on domestic abuse in Scotland (though a partner abuse module is incorporated into the SCJS), and challenges remain in terms of how domestic abuse is measured and understood.

The repeated and continuing nature of domestic abuse renders it difficult to accurately measure within surveys (Farrell and Pease, 2010), and these challenges are exacerbated due to the likelihood of domestic abuse being sustained in various different ways within, and following, a relationship:

> Accurate measures of the incidence of intimate partner violence are hampered by the nature of this violence: that it can take place over a long period of time and can involve various types of violent acts. Violence may permeate a relationship, or it may occur at a certain point in time, for example, when partners

are separating. It may be difficult for victims to enumerate each incident of violence, especially when these occur often (FRA, 2014, p. 42).

Nonetheless, while efforts to identify the prevalence of domestic abuse are likely to result in an under-estimation of the scale of the problem for these reasons, an analysis of ten separate domestic violence prevalence studies by the Council of Europe showed consistent findings: one in four women experience domestic violence over their lifetimes; and 6–10% of women suffer domestic violence in a given year (Council of Europe, 2002). These findings have since been replicated in other European studies (FRA, 2014). Hence, international research confirms that domestic abuse is a prevalent and persistent problem.

A growing body of national and international research also informs our understanding, not just of the extent, but also of the nature of the problem. In other words, who does what to whom, when, why and with what consequences (Hester, 2013). Existing research indicates that domestic abuse may first occur at different stages of a relationship and continue well beyond the relationship ending. In an EU-wide survey, 82% of women whose current partner was violent to them said that the first incident of physical and/or sexual violence occurred when they were living together (FRA, 2014). In the same survey, of women who had separated from a violent partner, 91% experienced violent incidents during the relationship, 33% also experienced violence during the break-up and around one in six (16%) stated that the violence continued or started after the break-up (FRA, 2014).

A wide range of behaviour constitutes domestic abuse. At its most extreme, this may result in severe injury or murder (Dobash and Dobash, 2015). While physical abuse may be the most visible or recognisable form of domestic abuse, sexual, emotional and financial abuse are equally damaging. Indeed, emotional abuse is a salient and arguably underpinning feature of this abuse though the dynamics of domestic abuse are known to vary over time within relationship and across different types of relationship. For example, in their research on domestic abuse in same-sex relationships, McCarry et al. (2006) found that, while sexual abuse was a notable risk for gay men, emotional abuse was more common within lesbian relationships.

Those experiencing domestic abuse report that the fear or threat of violence can be a greater concern than physical violence itself (Pain, 2012) due to the ongoing impact that this fear has on controlling victims' lives. Controlling behaviour has been found to be present in the majority of relationships where men are violent to their female partners (Hoyle and Sanders, 2000). Such behaviour may include name-calling, threats to hurt pets or other family members, isolation from friends and family, financial control and ongoing criticisms of the woman or her choices (Dobash *et al.*, 1996; Johnson and Sacco, 1995). The operation of such controlling behaviour has been well documented within feminist scholarship (Dobash and Dobash, 1979; Pence and Paymar, 1993; Stark and Flitcraft, 1996; Yllö and Bograd, 1988), most notably within the work of Evan Stark (2007; 2009).

For Stark, coercive control is a cumulative form of subjugation that uses a range of tactics – physical abuse alongside non-physical abusive behaviour such as threats, intimidation, stalking, psychological abuse, economic oppression and restrictions on liberty – that both isolate women and 'entrap' them in relationships with men by making them constantly fearful (Stark, 2007). A central feature is the focus on the (controlling) impacts of behaviour rather than individual acts.

The impact of domestic abuse

As discussed in subsequent chapters, the emotional, social and health impacts of domestic abuse on those who witness or experience it are profound. Attempts to understand domestic abuse that neglect impact (or perpetrator intent) by simply focusing on the acts perpetrated are of little value and risk generating spurious findings, which suggest that domestic or intimate partner violence experienced by men and women is at a similar level (Walby *et al.*, 2017). While it is acknowledged that both men and women may experience domestic abuse, research consistently highlights that victimisation varies by gender: namely, that women experience a greater range of abusive acts, more frequent abuse and are more likely to be injured as a result of the abuse (Dobash and Dobash, 2004; Walby and Allen, 2004; Hester, 2013).

The myriad ways in which domestic abuse impacts upon women, however, will vary. As Westmarland (2016, p. 16) notes, 'not all women are equal'; their varying social positioning, resources and experiences of other forms of oppression on grounds such as age, race, class, sexual orientation and citizenship status will affect their ability to endure and survive abusive relationships. It has been argued that knowledge and understanding of domestic abuse is heterocentric, making it more difficult for those in same-sex relationship to recognise their experiences as domestic abuse and access support or justice (Brown, 2008; Donovan and Hester, 2010), despite estimates that the level of domestic abuse within same-sex relationship is comparable to that in heterosexual relationships (Henderson, 2003). Meanwhile, it has been argued that the needs of younger and older women exposed to domestic abuse have been overlooked within some service responses (Hearn and McKie, 2010; Scott, 2004), particularly those of young transgender women (LGBT Youth Scotland, 2010). Where experiences of domestic abuse intersect with other forms of oppression, its detrimental impact is likely to be particularly acute. The related issue of forced marriage, most prevalent in South Asian and African families, intersects with wider experiences of racism; in these situations, experiences of domestic abuse must be considered as part of a multifaceted experience of abuse (Chantler *et al.*, 2009).

In summary, drawing upon qualitative research with those who have experienced domestic abuse has made a significant and meaningful contribution to providing an in-depth and nuanced understanding of the lived reality of domestic abuse and the impact that it has on the lives of the broad range of individuals and communities who experience it. This work can meaningfully complement, develop and inform the interpretation of survey data.

Interpreting research and statistical evidence through a gendered theoretical lens

It is apparent that the definition and measurement of domestic abuse are complex issues. One of the most contested aspects of understanding domestic abuse is found within the 'gender symmetry debate' where it is argued either that there is gender symmetry in IPV (i.e. that women are as likely as men to perpetrate violence against a partner) or that there is gender asymmetry in IPV (i.e. it is overwhelmingly men who perpetrate violence against women). This debate has been a site of some controversy across Western academic literature (Hester, 2013). Drawing upon an empirically informed theoretical framework to navigate this contested domain, however, can enhance understanding of contested study findings.

The work of Michael Johnson is particularly useful here. Controversially, Johnson has argued that much of the existing empirical domestic violence literature is virtually meaningless since it attempts to measure different types of violence, each with different psychological and social roots, interpersonal dynamics and consequences for the victim. Johnson (1995; 2008) developed an influential typology of IPV, which differentiates between three distinct forms of this violence: intimate terrorism (IT), situational couple violence (SCV) and violent resistance (VR). It can be argued that, without operationalisation of these distinctions, trends observed in domestic abuse data are reduced to a function of unknown combinations of the different types of violence.

Johnson defined IT as the attempt to dominate one's partner and exert general control over the relationship; domination that is manifested in the use of a wide range of power and control tactics, including violence. This form of violence is what is typically intended by terms such as 'domestic violence', 'wife beating' and 'spousal abuse'. Meanwhile, SCV occurs when specific conflict situations escalate to violence rather than being embedded in a pattern of controlling behaviour. VR, on the other hand, is used by someone experiencing IT to 'fight back'. Similar to IT, the violence involved in SCV and VR may be serious or even life threatening, but the distinction between the three types of violence is the relationship-level control context in which they occur, rather than the nature or frequency of violent acts. In the case of IT, one assault may be enough to establish a level of fear that allows the perpetrator to exert control almost exclusively by means of non-violent acts (Johnson, 1995).

Importantly, Johnson's work in utilising this typology to reanalyse existing survey data has shown that SCV in heterosexual relationships tends to be gender symmetric, whereas IT is perpetrated almost entirely by men. Johnson (1995) and Johnson and Ferraro (2000) contend that these distinctions are, therefore, essential to theorising and responding to IPV. Johnson's conclusions have been echoed in other work. Dobash and Dobash (2004) attempted to unravel the 'puzzle' of contradictory research findings on IPV by interviewing male and female partners in relationships where IPV was present. They conclude that their findings regarding the nature and consequences of women's violence make it impossible to construe the violence of men and women as either equivalent or reciprocal. Meanwhile, Griffiths (2000) found that, while men's violence to women is grounded in achieving power and control, women's violence to men is more commonly motivated by fear, self-protection and defence. More recently, Hester (2013) reported the findings of six-year longitudinal research analysing cases of domestic violence reported to the police in England with male and female perpetrators. Comparison of when men, women or both were recorded as perpetrators revealed significant differences: a greater number and severity of incidents were perpetrated by men and these incidents were more likely to involve fear and control of female victims. Where women were the perpetrators, they were more likely to use weapons (often in the context of self-protection) and have issues relating to poor mental health and alcoholism.

While Johnson's typology was initially developed by reviewing US-based survey data, it can usefully be transferred to data gathered in other jurisdictions. Applying Johnson's typology to the data reviewed earlier in this chapter would suggest that much of the data gathered through police statistics and crime surveys may represent SCV or VR, rather than IT, because of the decontextualised, incident-based, approaches to data collection. Viewing *Scottish Crime and Justice Survey 2014/15* (Scottish Government, 2016d) data through this lens may go some way to understanding findings which suggest that the incidence of IPV experienced by women and men is not entirely dissimilar, at 3.4% and 2.4% respectively. Commenting on prevalence data drawn from the Crime Survey for England and Wales, Myhill (2017, p. 42) describes the finding that 'one in four women' and 'one in six' men experience domestic abuse as 'hugely misleading'.

In England and Wales, the Office for National Statistics (ONS) has recently sought to improve measurement of abuse by commissioning a Domestic Abuse Statistics Steering Group. Two proposals have emerged from this group, and these are discussed by Walby *et al.* (2017) and Myhill (2017).

Firstly, Walby *et al.* (2017) propose a new methodological approach that would allow for more sophisticated measurement of physical violence and align this measurement with crime codes; doing so would, therefore, necessitate a helpful focus on 'intent' and 'harm'. Attention to gender – through a focus on victim and perpetrator gender, the relationship between victim and perpetrator, and whether the violence contained a sexual element – is an important part of this proposal. Walby *et al.* (2017) contend that this approach has the potential to mainstream gender into the measurement of domestic abuse.

Secondly, with regard to illuminating the gender dynamics of domestic abuse, Myhill (2017, p. 38) agrees that the approach advocated by Walby *et al.* (2017) would bring to light the disparities in the frequency and severity of violence perpetrated by men and women. However, as Myhill (2017) observes, this falls short of fully resolving the difficulty or revealing the gendered nature of domestic abuse. This is due to the suggestion by Walby *et al.* (2017) that conceptualisations of physical violence should not include non-violent forms of coercion. In effect, by excluding the coercive and controlling context that acts of violence may occur in, both the most serious forms of abuse and the primary perpetrators remain obscured (Myhill, 2017). Further, Myhill (2017, p. 38) warns that focusing on physical violence alone 'will, paradoxically obscure the gendered nature of abuse in other respects', including instances where an abused partner 'fights back' as an act of VR (Johnson, 2008). Drawing upon the concept of coercive control, Myhill (2017) argues that the current unsatisfactory impasse in the use of surveys to effectively measure domestic abuse can be overcome.

Conclusion

This chapter has illustrated the contested nature of understanding, defining and measuring domestic abuse, including divergences between legal, political and research definitions. Scotland's progressive gendered analysis of domestic abuse, which focuses on the relationship between current or former partners, builds upon our understanding of what it means to be a man or woman in society and how these roles are enacted in intimate relationships. It should also be acknowledged, however, that other characteristics such as race, religion, ethnicity, sexual orientation, age and disability will intersect and impact on how domestic abuse is experienced and responded to. These intersections, with some notable exceptions, remain under-researched.

Areas of contention and limitations of existing data about domestic abuse have been highlighted. Although police and crime survey data provides useful indicators of trends in reporting over time, their particular limitations lie with the 'snapshot' they provides in the measurement of a problem which is characterised by an ongoing and complex pattern of behaviour. Yet, as Walby *et al.* (2017, p. 5) contend, 'statistics matter' since they have the potential to 'entrench or contest social relations'. Recent academic contributions by Walby *et al.* (2017) and Myhill (2017) provide promising avenues through which to explore how survey methodologies can be improved; however, these frameworks have yet to be realised and there remains a lack of consensus between them.

Going forward, the integration of a gendered theoretical understanding of domestic abuse as a long-term pattern of controlling behaviour, with a methodology that moves beyond the 'snapshots' typically provided by incumbent approaches found within police statistics and other 'incident-based' studies, is required to fully understand domestic abuse. Johnson's theoretical framework, coupled with a conceptual understanding of the long-term nature of domestic abuse and its association with fear and control (Dobash and Dobash, 1979; Johnson, 2008; Stark, 2007), goes some way to navigating this contested terrain. Further, as discussed in Chapter 1, understandings of domestic abuse are most usefully set within a continuum of violence and abuse experienced by women and girls (Kelly, 1988), both within their individual relationships and across their lives. As will be discussed in the next chapter (Chapter 3), however, the adoption of a nuanced and gendered definition of domestic abuse sits uneasily with conventional approaches to policing domestic abuse.

Policing Domestic Abuse: The gateway to justice?

Oona Brooks-Hay

Introduction

For victims–survivors of domestic abuse, the police are a particularly important agency since they provide the entry point to the criminal justice system and have the power to offer protection from further abuse. They are also 'symbolically powerful' and a potential 'gateway to other agencies' (Groves and Thomas, 2014, p. 64). Yet conventional police responses to domestic abuse have attracted considerable critique, particularly from feminist authors and activists (Edwards, 1989; Dobash and Dobash, 1992; Hanmer and Saunders, 1984). Policing has traditionally been viewed as a hierarchical and masculine venture designed to fight crime (Fielding, 1994; McMillan, 2015), and as ill equipped to provide a sensitive response to victim–survivors of domestic abuse. It has also been argued that domestic abuse has been accorded low status within police forces and considered a distraction from 'real' police work (Edwards, 1989). Across a range of jurisdictions, the police have been critiqued for low levels of arrest (Edwards, 1989) and for failing to adequately pursue complaints of domestic abuse (Hanmer and Saunders, 1984).

In recent years, however, Scotland has witnessed considerable efforts to reform the policing of domestic abuse. Perhaps most notably, domestic abuse has evolved from a private matter to a very public one identified as an organisational priority for Police Scotland (Police Scotland and COPFS, 2017). This chapter will begin by outlining contemporary developments in policing domestic abuse, including Police Scotland's specialist response to domestic abuse, and the introduction of proactive measures designed to target perpetrators, enhance the safety of victim–survivors and their children and encourage reporting. While notable progress has been made in policing domestic abuse (e.g. clearer policy guidance, investigative protocols and the use of specially trained officers), there have been unintended consequences of policy and practice reforms, and it is argued that significant challenges remain, not least in terms of how the complexities of domestic abuse are addressed within a context of law enforcement. A key contemporary challenge, discussed in this chapter, concerns 'dual reports' of domestic abuse and the related issue of alleged female perpetration of domestic abuse. The chapter will conclude by reflecting on the potential implications of the new offence of domestic abuse for the policing of this crime.

A specialist police response to domestic abuse in Scotland

Policing in Scotland has recently been reconfigured through the introduction of a new national police service, merging eight regional police forces. Since its launch in April 2013, Police Scotland has identified domestic abuse as a key priority. This is, in part, a reflection of the way in which these crimes have become 'core business' for the police service. In contrast to other forms of violence, the number of domestic abuse incidents recorded by the police in Scotland has increased substantially over the past decade, as noted in Chapter 2. Rather than being viewed as an actual increase in domestic abuse incidents, this rise in the volume of incidents coming to the attention of the police is better understood as a reflection of changes to police practices and, relatedly, increased victim–survivor confidence in reporting their abuse. It is estimated that Police Scotland receives a domestic abuse report once every nine minutes, making it the biggest single demand on its time (Police Scotland, 2017).

The identification of domestic abuse as a policing priority has contributed to the establishment of a National Domestic Abuse Task Force staffed by specialist investigators to strengthen the police response to these crimes and target the most serious and prolific offenders. Meanwhile, the Domestic Abuse Coordination Unit (DACU) has been established to provide oversight of domestic abuse incidents at a local and national level. The DACU drives the domestic abuse agenda within Police Scotland, monitoring policy and practice, ensuring consistency and developing best practice (SafeLives, 2017). Specialist domestic abuse investigation units (DAIUs) have also been established in every local policing division across Scotland.

Within these units, specialist non-uniformed officers can provide follow-up advice and referrals to independent support agencies.

In Scotland, following a report of domestic abuse, police procedures are underpinned by a joint protocol, shared by the Crown Office and Procurator Fiscal Service (Police Scotland and COPFS, 2017). The joint protocol exists to identify best practice and ensure consistency of approach in the investigation, reporting and prosecution of domestic abuse cases. Initially introduced in 2004, the joint protocol has since been revised and updated in 2007, 2013 and most recently in 2017. In recognition of the serious and enduring impact that domestic abuse has on those who experience it, the joint protocol has the stated aims of treating all incidents as high priority and, reflecting a victim-focused approach, prioritising the safety and well-being of the victim. While the joint protocol states that a 'robust approach' is 'essential', assurances that victims and witnesses will be treated 'in a fair, sensitive and ethical manner' are offered (Police Scotland and COPFS, 2017, p. 2). In practice, this includes: ensuring the safety and well-being of victims and witnesses; thorough investigation of all incidents; taking appropriate action; actively pursuing offenders; and providing appropriate information and advice in relation to the support available from other agencies. Specially trained domestic abuse liaison officers (DALOs) are tasked with monitoring reported incidents, providing a personal contact point for victims, liaising with other agencies and explaining police and legal procedures. Hence, the role of the DALO represents a departure from conventional investigative police duties and is indicative of an increased emphasis on victim care in partnership with other specialist agencies.

Innovations in policing measures

In addition to the growth of specialist policing roles and units, a number of developments have occurred in relation to police measures for tackling domestic abuse. Internationally, there is some variation in the measures available, and Westmarland *et al.* (2014) note that more innovative policing practice than research-based interventions exists, particularly in relation to the policing of perpetrators of domestic abuse. Meanwhile, the most recent Her Majesty's Inspectorate of Constabulary (HMIC) (2014) inspection report in England and Wales illuminates the gaps that can exist between policy and police practice. Contemporary innovations in policing measures (disclosure schemes, alternative reporting mechanisms, multi-agency working and civil protection orders) are outlined below with particular reference to the Scottish context, and the evidence available about the use and effectiveness of these measures.

Disclosure scheme

Following similar developments in England and Wales, in October 2015 the Disclosure Scheme for Domestic Abuse in Scotland (DSDAS), informally known as 'Clare's Law' (after Clare Wood, who was killed by her partner in 2009), was rolled out nationally. The scheme aims to prevent the perpetration of domestic abuse by enabling people to request information from the police regarding their partner's violent history. Police Scotland (2016) has described the DSDAS as part of a long-term approach to supporting potential victims. Similar schemes have been introduced in the United States (US) and Australia. While they are seen to have some benefits, in common with other victim-focused initiatives they are considered controversial (Grace, 2015), not least since they do not guarantee victim safety in domestic abuse cases (Duggan, 2012) and may even have the effect of exacerbating the situation for women living with violence (Fitzgibbon and Walklate, 2016). The longer-term impact of DSDAS has yet to be evaluated, but in the first two years of its operation (2015–17) 2,144 requests for disclosure were received; this resulted in 927 people being informed their partner had an abusive past (Police Scotland, 2017). While this may be viewed as an important step towards preventing domestic abuse, there is some concern that such disclosures place the onus of responsibility for stopping abuse back on to victim–survivors.

Remote reporting

In comparison with other crimes, victims of domestic abuse are still among the least likely to report their victimisation (MacQueen and Norris, 2014). Efforts undertaken by Police Scotland to encourage victims to come forward include developing alternative routes to reporting domestic abuse beyond the conventional call to the police, though it is not currently known what impact these alternatives have had. Alternative reporting options include: an online domestic abuse form, which can be submitted to the police; and remote reporting sites where trained staff from partner agencies (e.g. Women's Aid, Rape Crisis and housing associations) receive reports and forward them to the police. Remote reporting was rolled out nationally in Scotland in 2013 and it offers victims of domestic abuse, witnesses to abuse or any person who has concerns for a victim of domestic abuse, the opportunity to report incidents in a confidential and supportive environment (reporters may remain anonymous if they wish). It is estimated that around one-third of incidents reported to the police are made by a third party (MacQueen, 2013 Scottish Government, 2017).

Multi-agency working

With regard to policing perpetrators of domestic abuse, partnership working is acknowledged as central to this process (Westmarland *et al.*, 2014; Burton, 2016; Davies and Biddle, 2017). Within Scotland, there has been a long-standing commitment to partnership working as a platform for addressing domestic abuse (Scottish Executive, 2000). The commitment has been reiterated most recently in the government's *Equally Safe* (Scottish Government, 2016a) strategy and the joint protocol between Police Scotland and COPFS subtitled 'In partnership challenging domestic abuse' (Police Scotland and COPFS, 2017). With regard to multi-agency and partnership working models, research evidence about effectiveness is limited although such approaches are widely recognised as good practice, which in turn contribute to robust risk assessment and safety planning (Brooks *et al.*, 2014; Davies and Biddle, 2017; Robinson and Payton, 2016).

Perhaps one of the most notable developments in partnership approaches relevant to the policing of domestic abuse is Multi-Agency Risk Assessment Conferences (MARACs). MARACs are primarily a police-led process which require meetings to be held across local communities whereby a range of statutory and voluntary agencies (e.g. police, health, child protection, housing services) share information and develop safety plans for high-risk domestic abuse victims (Cordis Bright Consulting, 2011). The MARAC approach was first developed in Wales (Robinson, 2004) and a review of MARACs conducted for the Home Office notes that available evidence on outcomes is relatively weak and that more robust evaluation is required (Steel *et al.*, 2011). However, based on the data available, the review concludes that MARACs have the potential to reduce re-victimisation and improve victim safety, while earlier research indicated that women valued the multi-agency support that they received through this process (Robinson and Tregidga, 2007). Further, Robinson and Payton (2016) observe that the MARAC approach has contributed to moving partnership practice from 'being ad hoc and discretionary to becoming routine and coordinated'. In Scotland, MARACs have been established as an important coordinated community response to ensure the safety of victims at high risk of serious harm. More than half (56%) of the referrals made to MARACs in Scotland are made by the police (Safe-Lives, 2017). It is estimated that a minimum of thirty-nine MARACs are required to meet adequate levels of provision in Scotland, though only twenty-eight are currently in operation with a further seven under development (SafeLives, 2017).

In addition to the use of MARACs, fourteen police-led Multi-Agency Tasking and Coordinating groups (MATACs) have been rolled out across Scotland as a means of targeting repeat domestic abuse perpetrators. Through partnership working, information sharing, tasking and coordination, the MATAC aims to identify and proactively target those domestic abuse perpetrators who pose the greatest risk of harm to victims and their families. Crucially, this reflects a victim-centred and perpetrator-focused approach to policing. It is anticipated that this approach will increase the number of domestic abuse related crimes detected and reduce the number of repeat victims and domestic abuse related homicides. Though this initiative has been in existence in Scotland for some time, it has not yet been formally evaluated. However, initial practitioner observations suggest some promising results in relation to reduced levels of reoffending for those perpetrators targeted by the MATAC.

In a recent evaluation of a MATAC in a police region in the north of England, Davies and Biddle (2017, p. 16) conclude that the MATAC had made 'significant progress' in relation to its objectives of preventing further abuse, improving victim safety, offender behaviour and criminal justice outcomes. Some concerns about the potential for a detrimental impact on victim safety as a result of a perpetrator-focused approach were raised within the evaluation, though Davies and Biddle found no evidence to suggest that the victims of targeted perpetrators were left unprotected; information sharing between key agencies and communication with victims about MATAC decisions were identified as key features of maintaining victim safety in this regard. Based on their evaluation of the MATAC, which draws upon the approach and risk assessment practices adopted in Scotland, Davies and Biddle (2017) recommend that the MATAC approach is continued and rolled out in other regions.

Protection orders

Civil protection orders are intended to prevent abusive behaviour from reoccurring rather than to punish a perpetrator for past behaviour. These orders are available in various forms in a range of jurisdictions including those within the UK, Europe, the US and Australia. The civil protection orders available to victims of domestic abuse in Scotland include: an interdict with no power of arrest; an interdict with power of arrest; and non-harassment orders. Police Scotland are responsible for the enforcement of these orders.

Since civil protection orders offer a means of addressing domestic abuse without invoking a criminal justice response, they may offer victims legal recourse without their partner or ex-partner being arrested and processed in the criminal justice system (Kethineni and Beichner, 2009). However, civil orders place the onus for making and funding these applications (either by using their own funds or accessing civil legal aid) on victims. If a civil protection order is not successful in protecting against further abusive behaviour, then criminal sanctions may follow the breach of a protection order. The Domestic Abuse (Scotland) Act 2011, for example, made it an offence to breach an interdict with a power of arrest in domestic abuse cases. Most recently, the Domestic Abuse (Scotland) Act 2018 requires the court, in every domestic abuse case, to consider whether the imposition of a non-harassment order is required to protect the victim from further harassment, as a matter of course.

Studies from a range of European countries (including Austria, Germany, Poland and Switzerland) demonstrate some positive effects of protection orders (Westmarland *et al.*, 2014). Granting these orders has some value in sending a clear message to perpetrators about the unacceptability and seriousness of their behaviour (Connelly and Cavanagh, 2007), and they can also provide a more rapid response to preventing further abuse than criminal proceedings (Ko, 2002). However, Burton (2016) raises the important question of whether increased reliance upon civil remedies represents a retrograde step in the policing of domestic abuse, by relegating it to a less serious non-criminal matter, rather than an innovation in policing.

With regard to the efficacy of protection orders in preventing reoffending, evaluation studies report varying levels of impact. In the US, studies indicate that between 23% and 70% of women victims report repeat incidents of violence despite having obtained a civil protection order (Holt *et al.*, 2003; Logan and Walker, 2010). Overall, however, the available evidence indicates that civil protection orders can be an effective mechanism for preventing further abuse, although the protective value of these orders may be hampered by barriers in accessing and enforcing them (Brooks *et al.*, 2014). The complexity of the process, time and cost may hamper applications for protection orders (Cavanagh *et al.*, 2003; Logan *et al.* 2004; Moe, 2000). Further, protection orders do not carry the same weight as criminal sanctions and may be viewed as 'merely a piece of paper' (Wallace, 2008, p. 247), unless there is an effective police response to breaches of orders.

Victims of domestic abuse may also apply for an exclusion order as a civil legal remedy intended to allow removal of the abuser from the home. In Scotland, exclusion orders were introduced through the Matrimonial Homes (Family Protection) (Scotland) Act 1981. Removing abusive partners from the home allows women, and any dependent children, to avoid the additional financial, practical and emotional stress associated with moving home, which may include the loss of support networks, employment and education (Brooks *et al.*, 2014). Although exclusion orders have been in existence for some time, there is little evidence of their use. An evaluation commissioned by SWA to assess how effective exclusion orders are in preventing homelessness of women living with domestic abuse highlighted the infrequent use of these orders; a request for an exclusion order was found in only thirty-four (1%) of the sample of family law cases reviewed (Avizandum Consultants and AAJ Associates, 2009).

Contemporary challenges

In addition to the inherently complex nature of domestic abuse, contemporary challenges to the policing of domestic abuse relate (ironically) to its increased political prioritisation, culminating in more 'robust' approaches and a higher volume of incidents coming to the attention of the police at a time of financial constraint. These challenges are explored below with particular consideration given to arrest policies and the implications they have for cases coming to the attention of the police in the first instance.

Pro-arrest policies

The political prioritisation of domestic abuse has facilitated a shift towards 'positive' or proactive police responses to domestic abuse. While this shift is broadly welcomed as an acknowledgement that domestic abuse is a matter of serious social and public concern, the adoption of a robust policing response to domestic abuse is not without consequences (both intended and unintended). Arrest policy is one area where this is particularly evident. A pro-arrest approach is now found in many jurisdictions, although some states in the US go further, by instating mandatory arrest policies (Kethineni and Beichner, 2009). These responses have been introduced largely due to concerns about case attrition at the police stage and police failure to arrest domestic abuse perpetrators (Buzawa and Buzawa, 2003). While mandatory arrest policies have been adopted in some US states since the 1970s, they have not been pursued in the UK, largely because of concerns about the removal of police discretion and, in turn, capacity to take into account the wishes of victims (Groves and Thomas, 2014). However, pro-arrest policies have been more widely adopted; in Scotland, where there is a sufficiency of (corroborative) evidence, the joint protocol (Police Scotland and COPFS, 2017) outlines a pro-arrest policy (irrespective of whether the victim is making a complaint).

Pro-arrest policies provide the potential for more perpetrators to be held accountable for their actions. However, an unintended consequence of pro-arrest or mandatory arrest policies, across a range of jurisdictions, is that more women are now being arrested as perpetrators of domestic abuse (DeLeon-Granados *et al.*, 2006). In Scotland, the proportion of incidents where women are recorded by the police as the perpetrators of domestic abuse, and men are recorded as the victims, has increased from 9% in 2002/03 to 18% in 2016/17. There is some concern that pro-arrest policies may result in both partners being arrested where there appears to be evidence of violent or abusive behaviour on the part of both parties in the relationship, irrespective of the dynamic underpinning these behaviours. Relatedly, concerns have been raised about the possibility that pro-arrest policies may have prompted an increase in 'counter-allegations'. This issue is explored in more detail below.

Dual reports or 'counter-allegations'

In Scotland (and elsewhere) there are growing concerns about counter-allegations and the related phenomenon of dual reports. Counter-allegations occur when perpetrators falsely claim that they are victims of domestic abuse in order to deflect legal proceedings against them and extend their control of their partners or ex-partners. Meanwhile, dual reports occur when both parties in a relationship are reported to the police as perpetrators of domestic abuse at the same time (and may include counter-allegations or incidents where a victim has retaliated). Reports of this nature are particularly challenging since police officers are confronted with two alleged perpetrators and victims, contrary to established understandings of domestic abuse as a crime perpetrated by one (predominantly male) partner against the other partner.

While research has usefully examined dual-perpetration of domestic abuse in England over time within relationships (Hester, 2009; 2013), with the exception of work by Brooks and Kyle (2015) no research has specifically addressed dual-report incidents that occur simultaneously in a UK context, or dual reporting specifically within a Scottish context. Using Scottish police data on domestic abuse over a one-year period (2012/13), Brooks and Kyle (2015) estimate that the police in Scotland record more than 3,000 dual-report incidents per year. This is a substantial number of incidents, and it raises questions about how the police (and the criminal justice system more broadly) manage these incidents.

The joint protocol (Police Scotland and COPFS, 2013; 2017) states that submission of a report to the procurator fiscal in respect of both parties should be avoided where there is reason to believe that a counter-allegation has been made. Further, following thorough investigation, every effort should be made to identify the primary perpetrator, looking beyond the current incident to consider the criminal history of both parties and the nature of the relationship between them. Only in limited circumstances (e.g. where both parties appear equally responsible or because of the severity of the behaviour) should both parties be reported to the procurator fiscal. Yet, Brooks and Kyle (2015) found that, in dual-report cases which proceeded to the procurator fiscal, the majority (69%) had a report submitted in relation to *both* incidents. Further, the proportion of incidents recorded as a crime and subsequently reported to the procurator fiscal in the dual-report sample (64%) was greater than the equivalent proportion for Scotland as a whole (39%) in 2012/13. While these findings might reflect the finding that a high proportion of dual-report incidents are reported by a third party and, therefore, have a witness to support the case, it may also suggest that there are challenges for the police in determining whether a counter-allegation is being made or whether one party may be acting in self-defence. This begs the question of how these incidents can best be understood and responded to.

On the basis of the quantitative police data analysed by Brooks and Kyle (2015) alone, it is not possible to ascertain whether dual reports are being made in the context of a counter-allegation, the actual dual-perpetration of domestic abuse or self-defence. Nonetheless, interesting observations about the nature of dual reports can be drawn from this data. Compared to other domestic abuse incidents recorded by the police in Scotland, dual reports are more likely to occur in current relationships, public locations, be reported by a third party and contain a public disorder element. This suggests that dual reports may be more typical of what Michael Johnson (2008) describes as 'situational couple violence' rather than 'intimate terrorism'. In other words, they are more likely to be based on a dispute between a couple that may have escalated (in public), rather than IT, which is characterised by the sustained exertion of power and control by one partner over another.

Drawing upon national domestic abuse statistics relating to perpetrator gender, Brooks and Kyle (2015) observe that women are the alleged perpetrator in more than five times as many dual-report incidents than in all other incidents reported to the police in Scotland. Only 3% of incidents with a male perpetrator and female victim occur within the context of a dual report, while 16% of incidents with female perpetrator and male victim happen within the context of a dual report. Hence, women are disproportionately represented as perpetrators in dual reports, and this may go some way to understanding why there has been an increase in alleged female perpetrators of domestic abuse within recorded crime statistics over time. In addition, a higher proportion of women involved in dual-report incidents were repeat victims (67%) than men (43%). Thus, women in the dual-report sample were over 50% more likely to have experienced repeat victimisation than male victims, and this gap grows as repeat victimisation increases: 26% of women had experienced six or more repeat victimisations compared to only 6% of men.

There was little difference in the type of incident recorded by gender although, interestingly, male victims were more likely to have sustained an injury (33% compared to 28% of female victims). This may be connected to the higher use of weapons where women are recorded as the perpetrator (11% compared to 2% of male perpetrators). Hester (2013) indicates that women's greater use of weapons is often linked to self-protection. This may suggest that some women within the dual-report study were acting in the context of 'violent resistance' (Johnson, 2008). Following research with the police in Northumbria, Hester (2011) contends that an understanding of the gender dynamics inherent in domestic abuse is central to the ability of the police to identify the primary aggressor, to question whether they had identified the correct perpetrator in incidents involving violence by women, and to contextualise retaliatory violence by women. Similarly, Myhill (2017) states that we must set violent acts in context and differentiate primary aggressor from primary victim if the true gendered reality of domestic abuse is to be revealed. The findings of Brooks and Kyle (2015) concur with these arguments and contribute to understanding the gendered dynamics of domestic abuse, though more (qualitative) research is required to fully comprehend this issue.

Policing a new criminal offence of domestic abuse

The introduction of a specific criminal offence of domestic abuse, as discussed in Chapters 2 and 4, is intended to provide a more robust response to domestic abuse and align the criminal justice response with the lived reality of domestic abuse as an ongoing pattern of abusive behaviour, rather than a one-off incident or a series of single incidents. However, it is likely that there will be challenges in the policing of the new offence. A primary concern will be how front-line police officers understand, recognise and evidence psychological and emotional abuse that amounts to coercive and controlling behaviour with detrimental consequences for individual liberty and autonomy (Stark, 2007) which appears, on the face of it, to be innocuous or trivial.

Research in other jurisdictions has confirmed that the challenge of identifying emotional or psychological abuse means the coercive and controlling behaviour is difficult to operationalise (Pitman, 2017). In relation to the new offence of 'coercive control' introduced in England and Wales, Myhill and Johnson (2016) suggest that officers will face challenges in relation to recording a 'course of conduct' with accuracy. Following an observational study of police officers responding to domestic abuse in England, they note that some officers 'lacked a nuanced understanding of the dynamic of coercive controlling abuse that would enable them to respond consistently and effectively' (Myhill and Johnson, 2016, p. 16). Additional training for front-line officers in Scotland may go some way to addressing this issue, and it has already been acknowledged that domestic abuse training is needed for all professionals who may be required to respond to domestic abuse, particularly police first responders, health and social care workers and members of the judiciary (SafeLives, 2017, p. 15; Burman and Brooks-Hay, 2018).

Difficulties in identifying what constitutes emotional and psychological abuse, however, extends beyond the parameters of the police response to the perceptions of victims-survivors and the public more generally. Importantly, these perceptions will influence the offences that come to the attention of the police. According to the *Scottish Social Attitudes Survey 2014*, people are less likely to recognise verbal abuse and controlling behaviour as being wrong and harmful compared to physical abuse (Reid *et al.*, 2015). Those experiencing these forms of abuse often struggle to identify and name what is happening to them as abuse, far less consider reporting to the police.

The proposed offence may also exacerbate the problem of dual reports and counter-allegations through the extended range of behaviour subject to criminalisation (including emotional and psychological abuse), which potentially creates a 'net-widening' effect and may inadvertently draw more women into the system as alleged perpetrators. While the risk of this happening may be mitigated by the requirement to demonstrate a course of conduct, the incorporation of the 'reasonable person' test and a focus on perpetrator intent within the new offence, any rise in the level of domestic abuse incidents as a result of net-widening is also likely to create challenges for the police response in terms of capacity and resources. It has been acknowledged by Police Scotland (2016) that the level of domestic abuse calls it receives on a daily basis already places considerable demands on its service.

Conclusion

The complexity of domestic abuse, coupled with its scale, renders it particularly difficult to resolve (Howarth and Robinson, 2016). Nowhere is this more evident than in its policing. To meet the formidable challenges presented by domestic abuse, considerable changes have been made to the resourcing and configuration of specialist domestic abuse police responses in Scotland and elsewhere. These structural changes have been accompanied by developments in police policy and practice, including some innovative measures in relation to reporting mechanisms, disclosure schemes, multi-agency working and civil protection orders. While they are considered to be promising practices, a number of these initiatives have yet to be evaluated, and understanding of their impact is therefore limited.

Challenges also remain in relation to how such measures, and the new statutory offence of domestic abuse, are implemented and there may be unintended consequences of doing so. While the new offence of domestic abuse has a powerful symbolic value in legally defining domestic abuse, its successful operation will be dependent on the ability of operational police officers to understand the nuanced (gendered) dynamic underpinning domestic abuse, particularly in dual-report and counter-allegation cases. Going forward, the way that the new offence of domestic abuse is policed will impact profoundly upon which cases enter the criminal justice system. The following chapter discusses the criminal justice response to domestic abuse and gives further consideration to both the aspirations and prosecutorial challenges associated with the new offence of domestic abuse.

CHAPTER 4

Domestic Abuse: A continuing challenge for criminal justice

Michele Burman

Introduction

The criminal justice system has long been criticised for a perceived inability to appropriately respond to domestic abuse, and a wealth of international research has highlighted the failure of criminal justice to meet the needs of victims and hold perpetrators to account (see, e.g., Edwards, 1989; Hoyle, 1998; Dobash *et al.*, 2000). While the criminal justice response has evolved from the days when domestic abuse was regarded essentially as a non-criminal matter, it remains subject to intense and critical scrutiny (Burton, 2008; Hester, 2013; Fitzgibbon and Walklate, 2016).

In Scotland, since the early 2000s, there have been several important developments: the introduction of a broad definition and a clearer formulation of the 'harms' of domestic abuse; the prioritisation of domestic abuse by Police Scotland and the Scottish government; the evolution of a distinctive multi-agency partnership approach; as well as policy innovation, legislative reform and specialised training for police, prosecutors and sentencers. Yet, despite high levels of political and media attention, the raft of policy and legislative reform, and successive well-intentioned strategic plans, domestic abuse remains pervasive in Scotland. As is the case internationally, academics, activists and criminal justice policymakers continue to grapple with the challenges posed by the complex nature of domestic abuse, as well as the demands presented by the growing volume of domestic abuse cases.

This chapter provides an overview of developments in the criminal justice response to domestic abuse in Scotland. It charts the most significant reforms introduced in Scotland: increased training and awareness-raising among criminal justice practitioners; developments in the prosecution approach; the introduction of the specialist domestic abuse courts; and the rolling out of perpetrator programmes. It dwells in particular on recent developments in relation to the creation of a new, bespoke offence of domestic abuse designed to better reflect the experience of victim–survivors. While this legislation represents one of the most radical attempts yet to align the criminal justice response with contemporary feminist conceptual understandings of domestic abuse as a form of 'coercive control' (Stark, 2007), this latest reform also brings with it considerable investigative and evidential challenges.

A More Robust Criminal Justice Approach
Prosecutorial policy and practice

Over the past two decades, there have been considerable efforts to improve the criminal justice response to domestic abuse in Scotland (Mackay, 2010; Burman et al., 2007; Brooks et al., 2014). Demonstrating a progressive approach in terms of understanding the dynamics and consequences of domestic abuse, Scotland's prosecution service – the Crown Office and Procurator Fiscal Service (COPFS) – has, since the early 2000s, introduced a raft of changes including a dedicated Victim Information and Advice (VIA) service, and a specialist response through enhanced training and guidance for prosecutors. Responding to concerns about the provision of information to victims in domestic abuse cases, the role of VIA is to keep victims updated on the progress of their case and, in particular, provide notification of the outcome of the first court appearance: for example, whether bail is granted and the terms of any special bail conditions. VIA also links victim–survivors with specialist organisations that can offer practical and emotional support, such as SWA. In a novel move, a dedicated lead national prosecutor for domestic abuse was appointed within COPFS, in 2013, to oversee the prosecution of domestic abuse cases, with a wide-ranging remit for the provision and review of guidance, policy and training.

Reflecting the national commitment to multi-agency working in relation to domestic abuse (discussed in Chapter 1), a key policy aim in Scotland has been to improve the coordination of information across the justice system to aid victims and respond to perpetrators, although to date the focus has been primarily on the criminal rather than civil justice dimensions. Emphasising the importance of a partnership approach, as discussed in Chapter 3, a Police/COPFS joint protocol outlines procedures and practices to be followed in domestic abuse cases, favouring a consistent and robust investigative, enforcement and prosecution approach (Police Scotland and COPFS, 2013; 2017). This joint protocol has the stated aims of treating all incidents as high priority. Where there is a sufficiency of evidence, there is a presumption in favour of prosecution. Somewhat controversially, particularly in cases where there is a reluctant complainer, there is a presumption against the discontinuation of proceedings even though a sufficiency of evidence remains. Where a decision is taken not to prosecute an accused, then COPFS is required under the Victims and Witnesses (Scotland) Act 2014 to inform the victim of the reasons for that decision.

The challenge of rising numbers

As highlighted in Chapters 2 and 3, Scottish government official statistics reveal a marked rise in the volume of domestic abuse incidents recorded by the police, with a concomitant increased proportion of cases referred to the procurator fiscal, alongside a corresponding fall in the imposition of police warnings and decisions to take 'no further action'.

Prior to the introduction of the Domestic Abuse (Scotland) Act 2018 (discussed later in this chapter), cases of domestic abuse were charged and prosecuted by means of the existing range of common law and statutory offences, including: common and aggravated assault; breach of the peace; stalking; vandalism; housebreaking; rape and attempted rape; murder or attempted murder; possession of an offensive weapon; and breach of a non-harassment order, interdict and bail which, if carried out by someone on their partner or ex-partner, could be classed as an incident of domestic abuse. These offences are recorded by means of a 'domestic' aggravator flag to reflect the additional information relating to the nature of the charge. There has been a marked rise in the numbers of charges with a domestic abuse aggravation reported to COPFS, from 27,100 charges in 2012/13 to 30,630 in 2016/17 (COPFS, 2017), and a correspondingly higher proportion of charges with a domestic abuse aggravator sent to court, with more than 85% of charges (26,157 out of 30,630) sent on to court in 2016/17 (COPFS, 2017). As discussed in Chapter 3, the majority of domestic abuse reports and charges involve female victims and male perpetrators, although there is an increased number of cases involving dual reports (Brooks *et al.*, 2015).

The Scottish government publishes statistics on criminal proceedings and convictions in the Scottish courts, and these reflect marked annual increases in the number of convictions in cases of domestic abuse. In 2014/15, there was a 14% increase in the number of offence convictions with a domestic abuse aggravator recorded, with 15,452 offence convictions, up from 2013/14 where there were 13,570 offence convictions; 2015/16 saw a very slight (1%) dip to 12,374 convictions although levels remain over 44% higher than in 2010/11, where there were 8,566 convictions (Scottish Government, 2017a). The key driver for the longer-term increases in convictions has been breach of the peace, particularly that involving 'threatening or abusive behaviour' or stalking, which accounted for 44% of domestic abuse convictions in 2015/16 (Scottish Government, 2017a, p. 33). The vast majority of those convicted are male (87% in 2015/16). Sentence outcomes have also changed, with 13% of offenders receiving a custodial sentence in 2013/14 compared to 5% in 2003/04.

While the Scottish government has posited that the longer-term increase in domestic abuse charges and convictions may be reflective of better recording of the aggravator and a greater confidence in criminal justice processes (Scottish Government, 2017a), there can be little doubt that this increase in recent years is just as likely to be driven by the demonstrably more robust approach to tackling domestic abuse taken by both Police Scotland and the COPFS. There is also little doubt that the increased volume is creating considerable pressures in the criminal justice system, where domestic abuse is rapidly becoming mainstream criminal justice business and posing a considerable resource challenge for criminal justice agencies.

The emphasis on robust criminal justice responses is echoed in the current Scottish government strategy on responding to violence against women and girls, *Equally Safe: Scotland's Strategy for Preventing and Eradicating Violence Against Women and Girls* (Scottish Government, 2014a; 2016a) with its ambitious priorities: that Scottish society rejects all forms of violence against women and girls; that they thrive as equal citizens; that interventions are early and effective and maximise their well-being and safety; that men desist from all forms of violence against women and girls; and perpetrators receive a robust and effective response. *Equally Safe* emphasises that criminal justice has a key part to play in addressing its priorities and pledged a commitment to a 'whole systems' review of the justice approach – including: consideration of the criminal law relating to domestic abuse (and sexual offences); provision of support for victims; and the impact of justice interventions in changing perpetrator behaviour and wider public attitudes (Scottish Government, 2014a) – along with an additional £20 million from the Justice portfolio budget to tackle all forms of violence against women and girls. There is far less emphasis on civil justice interventions in *Equally Safe*, a rather surprising omission given the policy aim of multi-agency working.

Aligning policy and law

While Scotland's adoption of a broad and gendered policy definition of domestic abuse to include physical abuse, sexual abuse, emotional abuse and other types of controlling behaviour has been celebrated as ground-breaking (Coy *et al.*, 2007), until very recently there has been no specific criminal offence or statutory legal definition of what constitutes domestic abuse in Scots law, to match the ground-breaking policy framework. As discussed earlier in this chapter, prior to the inception of the Domestic Abuse (Scotland) Act 2018, cases of domestic abuse were charged and prosecuted by means of a range of common law and statutory offences and the attachment of a domestic aggravator. This lack of a specific domestic abuse offence has been seen by some to contribute to the difficulties in providing an effective criminal justice response.

For some time, there have been concerns as to whether existing Scots criminal law recognises all forms of (non-violent) abusive behaviour that might constitute domestic abuse and (mirroring concerns elsewhere) whether the criminal justice focus on single *discrete* incidents rather than *patterns* of behaviour obscures the multifaceted nature of domestic abuse. Influenced by Stark's (2007; 2009) work on 'coercive control', which emphasises the importance of power and control in relationships characterised by domestic abuse, a range of women's sector organisations, criminal justice policymakers and practitioners coalesced in their call for law reform to ensure recognition of the complex dynamics of domestic abuse. In Scotland, the concept of coercive control was considered a means by which to recognise forms of abusive behaviour that may not be covered by existing law and shift the emphasis to patterns of behaviour (Scottish Government, 2015; SWA, 2014).

Triggering a fairly rapid set of developments, in 2014 Scotland's Solicitor General called for consideration of the creation of a bespoke offence of domestic abuse. Such an offence was considered necessary to properly reflect the experience of victims of long-term abuse, during which they are repeatedly subjected to multiple forms of abuse, including patterns of coercive and controlling behaviour, in order to make prosecution more effective (Thomson, 2014). Thereafter, the Scottish government proposed the introduction of legislation to create a new statutory offence of domestic abuse as a means of better reflecting the experience of victims, and ensuring more effective investigation and prosecution (Scottish Government, 2015). The consultation *'Equally Safe: Reforming the criminal law to address domestic abuse and sexual offences'* (Scottish Government, 2015) sought views on a range of changes to the law to strengthen the powers of police and prosecutors to tackle domestic abuse and sexual offences, including whether a specific offence of domestic abuse would improve victims' access to justice. Between December 2015 and April 2016, the government undertook a further consultation on a draft offence intended to cover the wide range of conduct that can constitute a pattern of abusive behaviour within a relationship and, in March 2017, the Cabinet Secretary for Justice announced the Domestic Abuse (Scotland) Bill proposing a specific offence intended to cover the wide range of conduct that can make up a pattern of abusive behaviour within a relationship, which is designed to criminalise a 'course of behaviour' involving abuse on at least two occasions (so single incidents are not covered, but would be by other existing laws). Additionally, for an offence of domestic abuse to have been committed, two other conditions must be met: the behaviour needs to be such that a reasonable person would consider it likely to cause the victim physical or psychological harm; and that the accused either intended to cause the victim physical or psychological harm, or else has been reckless as to the causing of such harm. Hence, the focus is on the behaviour of the alleged perpetrator rather than the victim's reaction.

Unlike the (more narrow) offence of 'controlling or coercive behaviour in an intimate or family relationship' introduced in England and Wales (Serious Crime Act 2015, section 76), which was intended to capture behaviour that was *not* covered by existing criminal offences, the Scottish approach – in its attempt to show a pattern of abuse and better reflect the experience of victims – is designed to cover behaviour which is *already criminal* as well as that which might not be covered by existing offences. While proponents welcomed the wide scope of the new offence, it arguably risks over-criminalisation – a criticism posed by senior legal figures and academics concerned at the potential net-widening effect of the new offence – arising from the range of behaviour potentially caught by the legislation, in the absence of further thresholds to reduce criminalisation (Burman and Brooks-Hay, 2018).

There are high aspirations for the new offence. The policy aim behind making it a criminal offence for a person to engage in a course of behaviour that is abusive of their partner or ex-partner is to ensure that Scots criminal law reflects a 'modern' understanding of the multifaceted nature of domestic abuse, and clarifies, for both victims and perpetrators, what constitutes criminal behaviour. However, like all law reform no matter how well-intentioned, it is likely to face challenges in implementation. There are likely to be difficulties around identification of subtle and insidious controlling behaviours, and apparent reluctance on the part of many victims to report domestic abuse (Burman and Brooks-Hay, 2018). Research in other jurisdictions has noted that coercive controlling behaviour has proven difficult to operationalise (Pitman, 2017) and recognise (Robinson *et al.,* 2017), not least because of the challenge of identifying emotional or psychological abuse.

The new offence carries with it the aspiration of facilitating a criminal justice response that is less incident-based and more appreciative of the ongoing patterns of behaviour which characterise abuse. It is clear that the implementation of this offence relies heavily on the ability of police to identify the presence of forms of coercive and controlling behaviour, and assess a pattern of behaviour. To do this correctly requires a shift from assessing a particular incident to one of recognising and interpreting a series of interrelated events. As argued in Chapter 3, for this to be realised, it is crucial that criminal justice professionals appreciate the complex nature of abusive behaviour, including the centrality of gender dynamics (Hester, 2011; Burman and Brooks-Hay, 2018) in order to understand the context in which it occurs. Indeed, Scottish research on health visitors' response to domestic abuse reveals a lack of understanding and confidence, a real reticence to engage even when women had been referred to them by the police, with some falling back on normative assumptions that reproduce the oppression of women (McFeely, 2016). Professional training and awareness-raising – with the aim of better serving the needs of victims, and improving prevention practices – are key.

There are also particular evidentiary barriers that will need to be surmounted to improve the investigation and prosecution process. A fundamental one will be proving an intimate relationship; there is a disconnect between the Act's definition of an intimate relationship and that outlined in the joint protocol. While there is a presumption in favour of the Crown that the relationship is deemed proven unless challenged, it would be difficult to establish if challenged. Second, in Scots law, the requirement of corroboration requires two different and independent sources of evidence in order to prove a crime. Although applied to all crimes, it is considered to increase the barriers to prosecution and conviction when applied to rape and incidents of domestic abuse that frequently occur in private. No matter how serious the allegation or how severe the consequences for the victim, if there is no second source of evidence to support an allegation of domestic abuse there can and will be no prosecution, and victims are effectively denied access to justice. While the intention of the legislation is that corroboration should become easier, in that a lesser offence could potentially be corroborated by a more serious offence if they form part of the same course of conduct, this could be perceived as an 'erosion' of the requirement and may raise concerns from those seeking to protect the rights of the accused. Notwithstanding, it is anticipated that there will be particular challenges in substantiating a 'course of conduct' of abusive behaviour rather than a single incident as well as corroborating emotional and psychological abuse, again due to its inherently private and individual nature (Burman and Brooks-Hay, 2018).

The Domestic Abuse (Scotland) Bill also introduced other important proposals beyond the definitional change, which are included in the new legislation. Notable is the inclusion of an aggravation in relation to a child, which is intended to ensure, first, that the new offence captures the seriousness of using children in the commission of domestic abuse and, second, reflects the harm that can be caused to a child who sees, hears or is present during an incident of domestic abuse. Notable too is the admissibility of the use of expert psychological or psychiatric evidence, relating to behaviour or statements made by the victim, for the purpose of rebutting adverse inferences made as to credibility or reliability, which is a notoriously difficult and pernicious problem in cases of rape and sexual assault (Burman *et al.*, 2007).

A key concern in the consultations and ensuing debates related to victim safety. Reflecting this concern, a new standard bail condition is designed to prevent an accused seeking to further their control by approaching their victim. In addition, courts are obliged to always consider whether the imposition of a non-harassment order is required to protect victims from further harassment so as to ensure their protection, and to have particular regard when sentencing for the need to protect victims from further offences by the offender.

Contemporary Criminal Justice Developments
Specialist domestic abuse courts

Specialist domestic abuse courts are now a feature in several jurisdictions. First introduced in the US and Canada in the early to mid-1990s (Hester *et al.*, 2008; Matczak *et al.*, 2011), and established in the UK in Leeds in 1999, numbers quickly proliferated across England and Wales. In Scotland, the first pilot specialist domestic abuse court was established in Glasgow in October 2004, with others following in Ayr, Edinburgh and Livingston. Glasgow and Edinburgh have dedicated domestic abuse courts, whereas Ayr and Livingstone have 'cluster' courts where all domestic abuse cases are heard on the same day. Specialist domestic abuse courts were created with the intention of addressing perceived inadequacies with the existing court process, in particular the lack of awareness of domestic abuse issues among criminal justice practitioners, and concerns about victim safety and support, as well as low levels of victim confidence and their apparent reluctance to engage with the criminal justice process (Cook *et al.*, 2004; Vallely *et al.*, 2005).

A shared aim of such courts is enhancing victim safety and support while holding perpetrators accountable for their actions; however, there are variations in the specialist models adopted (e.g. in terms of clustering of cases or fast-tracking of cases). Some courts deal only with either civil or criminal matters while others adopt an integrated approach to deal with both civil and criminal matters (Connelly, 2011); and there may be differences in terms of the remit of legal personnel involved and approaches to disposals (Robinson, 2007).

The specialist domestic abuse courts in Scotland, while not all the same, nonetheless share many features in common with similar courts in other jurisdictions in that they aim to: improve victims' experience of the criminal justice system; increase victim confidence and satisfaction with the criminal justice system; increase victim participation in cases; and reduce repeat victimisation and reoffending. But the Scottish courts are distinctive in their emphasis on the significance of multi-agency working relationships between the police, the prosecution and specialist domestic abuse service providers, and they reflect the policy aim to improve the coordination of information across criminal justice agencies. This again signifies the national commitment to partnership working to aid victims and to respond to perpetrators (Connelly, 2011, p. 110), which is also signalled in the Police and COPFS joint protocol for challenging domestic abuse.

Specialist domestic abuse courts are highly complex entities and, like other specialist forms of adjudication, involve elements of supervision, review and enforcement and require the close working and cooperation of a range of criminal justice, social work and third-sector professionals. Good working relationships are vital to their successful operation. In the Scottish domestic abuse courts, the multi-agency approach is reflected through the use of specialist trained prosecutors and sentencers, and the presence of independent domestic abuse advocates (IDAAs) provided by specialist, third-sector organisations such as ASSIST (Advocacy Support Safety Information Services Together), EDDACS (a bespoke advocacy service) and SWA. The provision of advocacy support encourages engagement with the court process, and also focuses on reducing risk and improving victim safety.

Recognising the inherent vulnerability associated with being a victim of such crimes, the Victims and Witnesses (Scotland) Act 2014 provides victims of domestic abuse (as well as victims of sexual offences, human trafficking and stalking, and all those under eighteen years old) with automatic eligibility to 'special measures' when providing evidence in court, such as screens in court and giving evidence remotely via video-link.

Unlike in England and Wales, where legal aid does not support a specialist domestic violence duty solicitor, the Scottish Legal Aid Board (SLAB) provides for a dedicated duty solicitor to be available.. The domestic abuse courts deal with all stages of cases including first appearance custody cases, intermediate diets, trials, reviews and deferred sentences. Sentencers maintain judicial oversight in sentencing and management and continue face-to-face contact with those who breach community-based disposals and are returned to court for re-sentencing. While there are tailor-made supervision programmes and perpetrator programmes (discussed below), there is not, as yet, judicial oversight in the form of reviews like there is in the specialist drug court, which takes a true 'problem-solving' approach (McIvor, 2009). Proper assessment of risk to victims, safety measures such as conditions that keep perpetrators away during the court process, and the consideration of non-harassment orders that allow ongoing protection after court proceedings have finished are crucial to ensuring an appropriate response to domestic abuse.

Specialist domestic abuse courts have been evaluated with regard to their implementation, process and outcomes, and research has identified a range of benefits. The Glasgow Domestic Abuse Court was subject to an evaluation in 2007, which was largely positive (Reid Howie, 2007); however, data on the impact of the courts on reoffending is limited. Despite the innovation presented by the domestic abuse courts in terms of evidence-gathering, preparation and procedure, there are very real and continuing concerns about the capacity of these courts to deal with the increased volume of cases and the significant length of time that cases take to reach conclusion (Robertson, 2014). A further concern relates to the relative lack of links between the criminal and civil courts in relation to domestic abuse cases. The lack of a joined-up approach is problematic here, especially with regards to issues relating to child custody and child contact – an irony given the government's emphasis on partnership working with other agencies. Increased understanding of domestic abuse, which has been largely developed in the context of a criminal justice approach, is reflected to some extent in the extensive statutory obligations on the civil courts to consider domestic abuse in child contact cases, yet there is concern that this approach is not working as well as it might (Morrison *et al.*, 2013).

Working with perpetrators

Widespread scepticism has accompanied claims about the ability of men who use violence to change their behaviour, and domestic violence perpetrator programmes (DVPPs) in particular have been subject to close inspection and strong criticism (Kelly and Westmarland, 2015a). While perpetrator programmes are used fairly extensively in the US and Australia, the research evidence as to their effectiveness has consistently shown mixed results (Eckhardt *et al.*, 2013). Studies deploy varying definitions and terminologies, because data is considered to be unreliable, and devising longer-term methods for effectively tracking impact remains challenging (Mullender and Burton, 2001; Morran, 2013). Kelly and Westmarland (2015b) argue that there has tended to be a rather limited view of potential 'success' measures, in that interpretation of what success means has ranged from an observed lack of future police involvement with men to the cessation of violence according to reports of current/ex-partners. Kelly and Westmarland's (2015a) Project Mirabal study aimed to understand what DVVPs contribute to coordinated community approaches to domestic violence and what 'success' means on a range of outcomes, and hence it moved beyond the criteria of measurement that simply viewed the end of physical violence as the desired outcome. Rather, the authors opted to explore what counts as 'success' from individuals' perspectives and developed meanings of success that go beyond just 'ending the violence' (Kelly and Westmarland, 2015b; Westmarland and Kelly, 2013).

Scotland first introduced perpetrator programmes in the 1980s with the inception of CHANGE and Lothian DVPP. The Caledonian System, first developed in 2004 and currently still in operation, provides an integrated approach to address men's domestic abuse and increase the safety of women and children through provision of a programme for men combined with integrated services for women and children. Men are referred to the Caledonian System if they have been convicted of offences involving domestic abuse, and are subject to a statutory criminal justice intervention: that is, a probation order (with condition); community payback order (with requirement); or a post custody licence. It currently operates across thirteen local authority areas and four community justice areas in five 'hub' sites. A key component of the Caledonian System is its inclusion of both a men's programme and a women's service.

Based on a cognitive behavioural model of change, the men's programme works with men over a period of two years, with the aim at reducing their reoffending while encouraging them to take responsibility for their actions and acknowledge their abuse and harm. It is highly structured, consisting of preparation, motivation and groupwork sessions and deploys a 'Good Lives Model' (GLM), strengths-based approach to offender rehabilitation, focusing on personal goals and the achievement of positive change (Ward, 2002; Ward and Gannon, 2006). Drawing on feminist theory, social learning theories and psychological theories, the Caledonian System advocates a multilayered approach to domestic abuse, recognising key individual formative experiences occurring within, and influenced or constrained by, historical and social contexts. As such, it deploys a nested ecological model in which to interpret and understand domestic abuse, and a framework through which change can be best understood. This model recognises that domestic abuse is multi-determined, and it provides a comprehensive explanation that includes elements of sociological and psychological understanding. The model also points to appropriate targets to address in work with men who abuse, such as attitudes to women and violence, as well as locating the work in its social and familial context (Burman and MacQueen, 2015).

Meanwhile, the 'woman-centred' women's service provides emotional support, safety planning and legal advice in order to protect women and children facing increased risks as victims. The model facilitates well-being and confidence-building by, for example, supporting women through the civil and/or post criminal conviction processes and by building their confidence. Women's safety and other needs (e.g. housing, financial, legal and post-trauma therapeutic intervention) are assessed so that relevant support may be put in place. In this context, multi- and intra-agency work – involving, among others, Police Scotland, COPFS and child protection agencies – is used to maximise safety, requiring sharing of case information.

The children's service aims to reduce the impact of domestic abuse on their lives, and includes a process of assessment of children's needs to address risks to their well-being and safety. A key role is to ensure the rights of the child and that their needs are met.; this incorporates ensuring that each child whose father (or mother's (ex) partner) is involved with the programme is kept safe, and has the opportunity for support. The service also aims to ensure that the range of services from different public and voluntary agencies working with children are experienced by children as integrated and well informed, and that bureaucratic and operational barriers are minimised (Burman and MacQueen, 2015, p. 12).

An evaluation of the Caledonian System found a range of positive impacts, including evidence that female partners feel safer, and that men who complete the programme pose a lower risk to partners, children and others by the end of the programme (Ormston *et al.*, 2016).

Conclusion

In this chapter, it has been argued that Scotland has witnessed some considerable advances in the response to domestic abuse, much of this occurring within a relatively short period of time. The Scottish approach to policy and legislation designed to tackle domestic abuse has focused primarily on criminal justice which, bolstered by political will and commitment, has produced considerable reform. There is little doubt that the reforms introduced by COPFS are noteworthy, and Scotland's commitment to specialised forms of adjudication as manifest in the domestic abuse courts are ground-breaking. So too is the strong commitment to multi-agency partnership working, and the close working arrangements between police, prosecution and third-sector organisations in the area of criminal justice. These developments have been strongly influenced by greater understanding of the complex and multifaceted nature of domestic abuse and, more recently, by the adoption of the concept of 'coercive control'. Significant statutory reform has led to the Domestic Abuse (Scotland) Act 2018, a bold and radical attempt to provide a nuanced approach to domestic abuse, but one which will likely face challenges in implementation.

Against the backdrop of a marked rise in the volume of domestic abuse cases coming to the attention of criminal justice agencies (Scottish Government, 2017), victim safety remains uncertain, and satisfactory justice outcomes for victims are far from guaranteed. Although the criminal justice response has become increasingly robust, with the focus on the provision of a consistent approach, perpetrator accountability still remains elusive. As Scotland has moved towards an increasingly tough and criminalising approach, critical questions remain about the 'bluntness' of the criminal justice system as an effective and sufficiently nuanced mechanism for responding effectively to a crime characterised by its complexity.

CHAPTER 5

Domestic Abuse and Health: Meeting the duty of care

Clare McFeely and Katie Cosgrove

Introduction

The preceding chapters discussed domestic abuse conceptually and at a national policy level, as a criminal justice issue. This chapter focuses on the impact of exposure to domestic abuse on the well-being of individuals and the ways in which professionals can best respond to the diverse care and support needs of survivors in the healthcare context. Domestic abuse significantly compromises the health of those who experience it, infringing their fundamental right to the highest attainable standard of health (WHO, 2016). The extent and impact of domestic abuse, and other forms of gender-based violence (GBV), are global public health problems (WHO, 2016). Health professionals have a duty to identify those at risk of harm and respond to their health and protection needs (NMC, 2015a; BMA, 2014). Challenges in developing an effective service response differ between countries reflecting the varying cultural and political responses to domestic abuse and provision of healthcare (Bacchus *et al.*, 2012; Kelly *et al.*, 2011). However, there are some commonalities: shaping an appropriate response within biomedically-focused services; sustaining changes in practice and organisational culture; considering the contested evidence on interventions; and navigating an evolving policy landscape. This chapter will explore these challenges, in particular the practice of asking about abuse, and present the Scottish system-wide approach to promoting an informed, person-centred and multi-disciplinary response within a complex health system.

Domestic Abuse: A Public Health Problem

The health consequences of domestic abuse are wide-ranging, affecting physical and psychological well-being (WHO, 2013). Poor physical health can result from traumatic injury (fractures, abrasions, bruising) and the longer-term sequelae of this such as arthritis, chronic pain and scarring or neurological consequences (e.g. seizures) (WHO, 2013; Campbell, 2004). Exposure to domestic abuse is also associated with chronic and long-term conditions such as gastrointestinal disorders, fatigue, fibromyalgia and cardiovascular problems (Campbell, 2004).

Specific health risks have been identified in relation to reproductive health and pregnancy. Women who have experienced abuse are more likely to experience gynaecological problems, are one and a half times more likely to have a sexually transmitted disease and are twice as likely to have a termination of pregnancy (WHO, 2013). Spontaneous abortion, haemorrhage, pre-term delivery and stillbirth are all associated with domestic abuse (WHO, 2013; Krug et al., 2002). Psychological consequences of domestic abuse include anxiety, depression, post-traumatic stress disorder, suicide ideation and attempt (Trevillion et al., 2012). Furthermore, women who have experienced domestic abuse are more likely to report behaviour that is harmful to health, such as smoking and alcohol misuse (WHO, 2013). Poor health diminishes women's opportunities for self-fulfilment and ability to engage with, and contribute to, society (Stark, 2007).

Children exposed to domestic abuse experience higher levels of depression, anxiety, psychological trauma, self-harm and suicide (Humphreys et al., 2008). Greater use of health services, increased medication, exacerbation of chronic conditions (e.g. asthma and eczema) and behavioural problems are also more frequently observed in children exposed to domestic abuse (Berman et al., 2011; Bair-Merritt et al., 2008; Holt et al., 2008; Humphreys et al., 2008). Given its health impact, which can persist long after the abuse itself has stopped (Pain, 2012; WHO, 2005), women and children exposed to domestic abuse are likely to be in contact with NHS services although their experiences of abuse are rarely recognised by the health professionals they encounter (Feder et al., 2009). Indeed, Walby (2009) estimates the financial cost of domestic abuse to health services as £1.73 billion. Thus, there is a clear role for health professionals to identify and address domestic abuse.

Duty of Care

In the UK, health professionals have a professional obligation to protect and promote the rights of those in their care (Beauchamp and Childress, 2013; DoH, 2010). This is reflected in health professions' codes of conduct, where responsibility to identify, protect and support those at risk of harm is clearly stated (HCPC, 2016; NMC, 2015a; GMC, 2013). Often, protection of those experiencing abuse is explicitly stated (NMC, 2015b; BMA, 2014).

Despite such obligations and the plethora of evidence on the health impact of abuse, research consistently finds that survivors of abuse are disappointed with the response of health professionals (Keeling and Fisher, 2015). As a universally accessible service, healthcare providers are in a unique position to engage with survivors yet they commonly cite time constraints, fear of being intrusive or of making things worse, and uncertainty about dealing with disclosures as impediments to raising the issue with patients (Feder *et al.*, 2009). Lack of confidence or the personal values of practitioners may further limit fulfilment of this duty of care (Virkki, 2015; Taylor *et al.*, 2013; Feder *et al.*, 2009).

Medicalising Domestic Abuse

Individual practitioners' reluctance to engage with domestic abuse is supported institutionally by the traditional biomedical model of healthcare delivery. This model focuses on biological determinants of illness (injury, infection and inheritance) and is the dominant model of healthcare in Europe, North America and Australia (Alonso, 2004). Despite established evidence on the social determinants of health (Wilkinson and Marmot, 2003), this model disregards factors such as social context and inequality, focusing instead on health consequences. 'Medicalisation' of domestic abuse ignores the actions of the perpetrator and the lived experience of the survivor. This is illustrated in the use of 'disembodied' language, described by Warshaw (1996): for example, recording injury being due to a hit with a fist, rather than being a hit by a person. Without consideration of an abusive partner, health professionals can assign responsibility for injury or associated conditions, and ultimately for the abuse, on the victim (Virkki, 2015; Williamson, 2000). Efforts to improve the health service response must accordingly address both individual and structural barriers.

The nature of health service delivery in Scotland is changing amid the narrative of a 'mutual NHS' (Scottish Government, 2007). Central to this is delivery of patient-centred care which includes consideration of contextual and biomedical factors, alongside clinical evidence, as well as health professionals adopting an empowering and facilitative role to support individuals to make decisions about their care (Scottish Government, 2010). This approach provides an opportunity to engage with survivors of domestic abuse (and the research in which they have participated) to identify a range of health service responses appropriate to individual experiences of domestic abuse.

NHS Scotland

As described in Chapter 1, health is a devolved matter, and health-related legislation is the responsibility of the Scottish Parliament (Scotland Act 1998). Decisions regarding funding allocation and monitoring of healthcare provision are made centrally by the Scottish Government Health Directorate (SGHD).

The vast majority of healthcare is provided free at point of access and is funded through taxation, although private healthcare providers are available. Services are delivered through fourteen territorial NHS Boards. In addition, there are eight 'special' NHS Boards, which provide a Scotland-wide service (e.g. the ambulance service). NHS Boards directly deliver the majority of healthcare, thus removing competition, reducing the number of potential providers and facilitating the development of a consistent, national approach. This contrasts with the commissioning system introduced in NHS England, where third-sector and private healthcare providers tender to deliver healthcare (Health and Social Care Act 2012). The provision of healthcare in Scotland continues to evolve with the establishment of joint Health and Social Care Partnerships within each local authority, which have responsibility for primary care and social care services. This has substantially changed management and funding structures, with greater decision-making powers devolved to local management boards (Scottish Government, 2016b).

Evolution of the NHS Scotland Response to Domestic Abuse

The debate on the role of the NHS around domestic abuse has advanced over the last twenty years from focusing on whether it is an issue for healthcare (BMA, 1998) to how best we can respond. In Scotland, efforts to drive change included early calls for a coherent NHS response (Scottish Needs Assessment Programme, 1997) and issuing national practice guidelines to NHS Boards. These documents supported individual clinicians and managers working across the NHS in Scotland to progress work within their own areas. The establishment of a National Domestic Abuse and Health Network linked these individuals and facilitated sharing of good practice, protocols and development of training resources between areas. Since implementation of the guidelines was neither mandatory nor monitored, their impact was diluted and the dependence upon committed individuals proved insufficient to effect the transformation required across the complex systems of the NHS.

In 2007, two national developments facilitated a change of approach by the SGHD; principally the government's strategic shift in focus from domestic abuse to the wider spectrum of VAW (Strategic Framework on Violence Against Women, later published as 'Safer Lives: Changed Lives' (Scottish Government, 2009)) and the work on producing the National Domestic Abuse Delivery Plan for Children and Young People (Scottish Government, 2008a). To meet their demands for a proactive and effective health service contribution, NHS Scotland appointed a National Gender Based Violence and Health programme manager to lead this process. To inform and shape this work, the programme manager sought the views of NHS Boards. All articulated a readiness to improve responses to GBV but reported feeling overwhelmed by the scale of the challenge and unsupported at a policy level. Noting the multiple points of entry to the NHS, through planned and unplanned care, and the magnitude of workforce development required they stressed the need for direction and clear priorities to progress work in this area.

Thereafter, a three-year national programme of action was devised and issued to NHS Boards in 2008 (Chief Executive's Letter 41 (CEL_41), (Scottish Government, 2008b)). Its overarching aim was 'to adopt a systems approach to ensure that the NHS in Scotland fully recognises and meets its responsibilities around gender-based violence as a service provider, employer and partner agency' (Scottish Government, 2008b, p. 2). The key objectives of CEL_41 were to improve identification of abuse, increase institutional capacity to respond, integrate GBV into key strategic frameworks and enhance multi-sectoral collaboration. CEL_41 sought to redefine GBV as core business and establish an organisation-wide infrastructure to support and sustain change. Integral to achieving this was ownership and accountability at board level, and each Board was directed to appoint an operational lead to develop an action plan in line with the national priorities, and to manage implementation. Nationally, the monitoring of the programme was linked to the National Domestic Abuse Delivery Plan for Children and Young People (Scottish Government, 2008a) and ultimately reported to the Cabinet Secretary at Scottish government. In keeping with its emphasis on demonstrating tangible, sustainable progress over three years, the programme set out four key deliverables:

- routine enquiry of domestic abuse in maternity, health visiting, substance misuse, emergency department, mental health and sexual health services;
- dissemination of health guidance on the spectrum of abuse covered by GBV to health staff;
- development of an employee policy for staff who are victims, survivors or perpetrators of abuse;
- enhanced collaborative working with other agencies.

A national GBV team was appointed to support development and implementation of action plans and policies, establish research evidence and monitoring systems, and seed training materials and sessions within Boards.

Routine Enquiry of Domestic Abuse

When, how and whether to ask patients routinely in healthcare settings about domestic abuse has been a contested issue for some years. Inclusion of domestic abuse in the assessment process was advocated long before its introduction in Scotland (RCM, 2006; Taket, 2004; RCOG, 1997). Although research indicates that women want to be asked about abuse and that it increases identification and disclosure while reducing stigma associated with abuse, the merits of screening as an appropriate healthcare practice continue to be debated (Feder *et al.*, 2009). As the cornerstone of the GBV programme, the introduction of routine enquiry represented a paradigmatic shift in practice in an area where controversy abounds. It is worth, therefore, outlining the rationale for its adoption and the ways in which this diverges from the common perception on screening.

First, a note on terminology. The literature variously references 'universal screening' (asking all service users regardless of health setting), 'selective screening' (asking an identified high-risk group e.g. pregnant women) and 'routine enquiry' (O'Doherty *et al.*, 2014; Feder *et al.*, 2009). Screening is a population-based intervention to identify disease in the latent or asymptomatic phase, and involves application of a standardised question to everyone meeting the criteria. Applied to domestic abuse, screening does not consider the context in which such abuse occurs and so cannot differentiate between women living with coercive control, Situational Couple Violence (see Chapter 2) or those continuing to experience health consequences of past abuse (Taket, 2004). Routine enquiry, by contrast, allows flexibility in how the question is asked, recognising that, while any experience of abuse can be detrimental to health, the responses required will differ considerably.

In NHS Scotland, routine enquiry of domestic abuse was introduced in a specific, targeted manner to improve assessment and care. Settings were identified where there is a disproportionately high level of abuse-related presentations – mental health, maternity, health visiting, sexual health, substance misuse and emergency departments. Routine enquiry was limited to asking all new female patients, at the initial stages of service engagement, whether they had experience of domestic abuse. Questions were incorporated into initial assessments to emphasise that knowledge of experience of domestic abuse is essential health information. Within mental health and substance misuse, routine enquiry of childhood sexual abuse (CSA) of all new service users (male and female) was introduced, given the prevalence of abuse within those service populations. Crucially, routine enquiry in and of itself was not proposed as adequate in dealing with domestic abuse. Rather, it was designed to promote early and effective identification and intervention to support and protect women experiencing abuse.

In contrast to screening, routine enquiry is best described as part of the diagnostic process. Facilitating disclosure enables a complete understanding of the genesis of some health conditions, essential for accurate diagnosis and suitable treatment (Taket, 2004). Concomitantly, a failure to enquire may prevent professionals from addressing a woman's primary reason for presentation and, potentially, the greatest risk to her well-being (Warshaw, 1996). Furthermore, incomplete assessment could introduce additional harm as a consequence of inappropriate or unnecessary treatment such as overprescribing of medication (NICE, 2014; Humphreys and Thiara, 2003). Indeed, the potential for health professionals to exacerbate survivors' experience of abuse is a relatively neglected issue throughout the discussion.

At the heart of the ongoing debate is whether or not enquiry improves health outcomes for women, with some arguing that there is, as yet, insufficient evidence of health gain to support screening (Feder *et al.*, 2009; Wathen and MacMillan, 2003). This argument focuses on the lack of data on positive health outcomes and conflates enquiry with the responses that follow, obscuring the qualitative benefits of enquiry. It also does not address the reality that the process of living in an abusive relationship, exiting the relationship and engagement with supports are non-linear. In some instances, the full health impact of abuse will not become apparent until the abuse has ended, and health, particularly psychological health, may worsen in the short-term following separation (Pain, 2012; McCloskey *et al.*, 2006).

Importantly, given the behaviours perpetrated as domestic abuse (physical, emotional, sexual) and wide-ranging consequences, each disclosure will require a unique response. For example, a woman who has recently begun to experience abuse may have different support needs to a woman who has endured coercive control over twenty years. Consequently, standard outcomes cannot be applied to different levels of need. The biomedically focused concept of evidence, based on narrowly defined benefits in relation to mortality and morbidity, concentrates on what can be controlled and counted and cannot fully evaluate public health interventions (Millward *et al.*, 2003; Malterud, 2001), such as routine enquiry. Similarly unhelpful are proxy measures, such as a reduction in violence, in interventions designed for the victim of abuse rather than the perpetrator (Campbell *et al.*, 2009). A biomedical focus has, to some extent, obscured the health professionals' first responsibility to protect and do no harm, and it ultimately ignores the wishes of survivors of abuse who should be partners in mutual health-care design. Failing to ask about abuse may also cause harm through normalising or ignoring women's experience of abuse. Inadvertently, health professionals can collude in the secrecy that surrounds abuse and, by failing to facilitate disclosure, reinforce coercive control tactics used by abusive partners, such as undermining women, reinforcing a belief that they are worthless and that 'no one can help you' (Keeling and Fisher, 2015). Although echoing concerns about screening, the National Institute for Health and Care Excellence (NICE) endorses the Scottish approach, advocating that:

> [s]taff in antenatal, postnatal, reproductive care, sexual health, alcohol or drug misuse, mental health ... services ask service users whether they have experienced domestic violence or abuse ... [as] a routine part of good clinical practice, even where there are no indicators of such violence and abuse (NICE, 2014, p. 13).

Implementation and Impact

In view of the wide-ranging aims of CEL_41, the national team utilised a range of evaluation methods to assess the implementation and impact of the programme (Scottish Government, 2012a). This included a process evaluation and routine monitoring data (Scottish Government 2012a), evaluation of the training programme (National GBV and Health Programme, 2011), gathering service user views on routine enquiry (National GBV and Health Programme, 2012) and gathering the views of NHS Board leads on implementation, conducted by an independent organisation (Blake Stevenson, 2011). As anticipated, the introduction of routine enquiry was challenging; although broadly supported, it was not universally welcomed or understood and required ongoing negotiation, persuasion and support (Blake Stevenson, 2011). NHS Boards leads reported that many operational aspects were time-consuming: for example, identifying and training staff affected by routine enquiry; negotiating across services on phasing in change; recording guidance; sharing protocols; and agreeing reporting mechanisms (Blake Stevenson, 2011). Of critical importance in supporting these processes was the input from the national team. Three regional advisors and a data and performance manager helped navigate NHS Boards through unfamiliar territory, alleviating concerns about the demands of routine enquiry and the logistics of working across services. A national GBV reference group brought together operational leads and the national team to discuss progress, enhance collaboration and promote consistency of approach. The accountability associated with the GBV programme, in which local ownership and governance were realised in every Board through establishment of a system-wide infrastructure to develop and oversee implementation of action plans, also proved to be a crucial ingredient in engaging more reluctant actors in Boards (Blake Stevenson, 2011).

The imperative of linking training to practice, especially when practice environments do not support or promote practice change, is well evidenced (Taket, 2004). Training for all staff undertaking routine enquiry was, therefore, mandatory prior to its introduction, and was delivered to whole teams to maximise a shared approach and minimise attenuation of training gain. Training covered the dynamics of domestic abuse and coercive control, health impact, trauma-informed care, role play on asking about abuse and appropriate responses to disclosure, safety planning and advocacy (NHS Scotland and Scottish Government, 2011).

Within the initial three years, more than 3,000 staff were trained. A response rate of 78% was achieved from the pre- and post-training evaluation questionnaire (Scottish Government, 2012a, p. 12). Findings indicated that training increased support for the practice of routine enquiry and confidence to both ask about and respond to abuse. Self-reported confidence in asking about domestic abuse rose from 40% (prior to training) to 90% (post-training). Similarly, those stating they had knowledge and skills to respond to disclosure increased from 33% (pre-training) to 85% (post-training). Participants described the training as a 'good grounding' and even experienced participants stated that it encouraged critical reflection on existing practice (Scottish Government, 2012a).

Focus groups were conducted within six months of the training sessions, with staff from a range of clinical settings, across eight board areas with a total of seventy-five participants (National GBV and Health Programme, 2011). Findings indicated that some resistance to routine enquiry persisted, particularly in mental health services. However, many participants reported a growing confidence in asking about abuse, with full acceptance and implementation in maternity services indicating a sustainable change. Progress in Accident and Emergency stalled because of a decision by the Royal College of Emergency Medicine (RCEM) (Scotland) to oppose the introduction of any population-based screening within emergency departments. However, training was delivered to staff within these departments and selective enquiry of abuse continues.

Access to health data was an intractable issue throughout this work. The range of systems for capturing data, and an inability to retrieve data, are ongoing issues for services, not just in relation to GBV. Frustratingly, this means that monitoring data do not reflect the structured and systematic approach to implementation of routine enquiry. However, some Boards have incorporated the core dataset into existing systems and are monitoring the identification of abuse for the first time in NHS Scotland (Scottish Government, 2012a). Local reports from one NHS Board stated that routine enquiry had been achieved in 31% of mental health and substance misuse service assessments, resulting in more than 2,000 disclosures of domestic abuse, sexual abuse in childhood and other forms of GBV not included in the routine enquiry questions. A second health board reported that routine enquiry occurred in 30% of assessments in substance misuse services and that 30% of those asked disclosed experience of domestic abuse and/or sexual abuse. Routine enquiry was introduced in a specialist health service for people experiencing homelessness by a third NHS Board, which asked two-thirds of new service users and found almost three-quarters (72%) of women disclosed experience of domestic abuse. This snapshot of activity illustrates the incremental approach of the programme and, importantly, the willingness of survivors to disclose.

The national team conducted a small evaluation with a convenience sample of fifty-five people exiting their first appointment at maternity, sexual health, substance misuse and mental health services in five NHS Boards (over twenty-two sessions) (National GBV and Health Programme, 2012). Routine enquiry was achieved in two-thirds of these sessions. All but one participant stated it was acceptable to ask, and 88% stated it was acceptable to ask on more than one occasion. Indeed, service users responded positively to the practice (National GBV and Health Programme 2012):

> 'I would have loved someone to ask me that before' (substance misuse service user)

A subsample of substance misuse service users (n=11) were asked about the acceptability of enquiry of CSA and involvement in prostitution. All agreed that it was acceptable to ask about prostitution, and all but one agreed that asking about CSA was acceptable. Again, this is a snapshot but it indicates that enquiry about other forms of abuse may be as acceptable as asking about domestic abuse in some settings.

Some areas exceeded the requirements of the GBV programme. One operational lead, anticipating that routine enquiry would increase disclosures of abuse across services, adapted policies and guidance for GPs and the wider primary care team and identified 'champions' to deliver ongoing support to colleagues. Early fears of being 'swamped' with additional disclosures were allayed, reducing practitioners' anxiety about their ability to respond appropriately as illustrated by the following quotes from evaluation focus groups (National GBV and Health Programme, 2012):

> 'Initially we did think there would be huge knock-on effects with other agencies, like psychology referrals would be sky high [...] but that doesn't seem to be the case' (mental health staff focus group).

Nonetheless, the discomfort for some staff remains, underscoring the need for support in ensuring consistency across services:

> 'They've all disclosed something and that's causing problems in other ways ... and it's an issue for me that I'm feeling now, I'm starting to retract. I cannot ask everybody because we don't have access to the resources that I think are required' (mental health staff focus group)

The evaluation revealed a significant shift both in terms of expectation of service responses to survivors and acceptance of routine enquiry as standard practice. The programme has thus had a transformative role in embedding abuse as core business of key services within NHS Scotland. In evaluation interviews, operational leads described a 'culture shift' in management and health professionals' views on their role in supporting survivors of GBV and stated that the national leadership allied with specific demands on Boards and clear accountability processes provided 'visibility and gravitas' for this work (Scottish Government, 2012a, p. 14).

With a workforce of more than 155,000 staff, NHS Scotland has a responsibility to promote the welfare of its staff. An important and innovative requirement was for a national employee policy on GBV to support staff with experience of abuse and to address the behaviour of alleged perpetrators. This was developed in collaboration with management and unions and now forms part of the employment contract for all employees (Scottish Government, 2011). All Boards adapted this for local use (retaining core provisions), and the national team provided training for managers to support implementation.

Sustainability

CEL_41 covered the period 2008–11. In 2012, the Director General of NHS Scotland directed all Boards to continue implementation of its key deliverables and, thereafter, embark on a process of continuous quality improvement (Scottish Government, 2012b). Although funding for the national team ended, the programme manager post continued and was transferred to NHS Health Scotland, a national board which addresses health improvement and inequalities, and which assumed leadership of the work. Despite the reduction in resources, and absence of formal monitoring, Boards have retained their infrastructure, using this as a platform to progress work on broader GBV issues such as sexual violence, stalking, female genital mutilation, forced marriage and human trafficking. The national GBV reference group continues to meet, providing a conduit for operational leads to influence policy and share practice.

Routine enquiry is now accepted as part of standard practice, and is integrated into key policies: for example, in the national standards for substance misuse services; maternity records; and the Universal Health Visiting Pathway. The last extends routine enquiry to completion of a structured risk assessment (SafeLives, 2014) for which further training is mandatory. Multi-agency work has also been strengthened. Innovative developments include collaboration between health services, third sector, and higher and further education to deliver undergraduate training on GBV. Furthermore, across NHS Boards health professionals engage with colleagues from partner agencies through MARACs and the Safe and Together Model (see Chapter 7).

The Gender Based Violence and Health programme continues within a landscape of policy change, some of which complement and support development of the health service response to GBV. The newly formed Health and Social Care Partnerships have a foundation in a social model of health more suited to recognising and responding to survivors' experiences.

International developments continue to influence developments in Scotland. In 2016, the World Health Assembly (WHA) approved a global action plan to strengthen the health sector contribution to ending violence against women and girls, and urged individual countries to adapt the plan to their national context. NHS Health Scotland is benchmarking progress against the WHA plan and outlining actions needed to fulfil a commitment to this and to *Equally Safe* (Scottish Government, 2014a). These priorities, alongside those identified by Boards, Health and Social Care Partnerships and service users of NHS Scotland, will inform the future direction of NHS Scotland on GBV.

Conclusion

Domestic abuse is a profound public health issue with considerable implications for health and healthcare. Early identification, assessment and intervention through the provision of skilled and attentive services reduce harm, improve health and are cost-effective.

Appreciation of these realities, coupled with the recognition that the onus for effecting change cannot solely rest with individual practitioners, provided the impetus for the national Gender Based Violence and Health programme in Scotland. The systems approach of CEL_41 represented a bold departure from established practice. Underscoring the shared ownership and responsibility across the NHS, it set out an ambitious programme for addressing GBV as service providers, employers and partners. Key to this was the clear direction and lines of accountability set out by the SGHD, providing NHS Boards with identified priorities and expectations on how these would be delivered.

A constellation of factors supported the development and implementation of CEL_41: political support, national leadership and the formation of a national team. It emboldened and supported those who had been working to progress this issue within the NHS, and also engaged with managerial and clinical staff previously uninvolved with the agenda. This local leadership was crucial for the programme's success. Routine enquiry provided a central focus for the work representing a paradigmatic shift in practice that was resisted by some but not derailed. Unevenness remains in its application across the country, and there is a continuous challenge in relation to information systems and the changing structure of service provision.

The lasting impact of the CEL_41, however, is in the cultural change it engendered within NHS Scotland. Routine enquiry has been embedded within services, and responding to domestic abuse and other forms of GBV is regarded as core business for the health service. While much still remains to do, the fundamental shift in how NHS Scotland understands and articulates its role is undoubtedly its most significant accomplishment. In the following chapter, the need for holistic organisational and cultural reform is discussed further by Lombard and Harris in relation to education and its pivotal role in addressing domestic abuse.

CHAPTER 6

Another Brick in the Wall? Preventative education in Scottish schools

*Nancy Lombard and Roy Harris**

> The earlier that there is a shift in discriminatory cultures, attitudes and behaviours the better, and primary and secondary schools are key settings for early intervention … Education professionals therefore have a huge opportunity to lead the way in attitudinal change, being in a prime position to nurture the next generations on positive gender roles and healthy, equal relationships from an early age (Scottish Government, 2014b, p. 24).

Introduction

This chapter examines the role of preventative education in primary and secondary schools in Scotland in relation to domestic abuse. According to Bigler *et al.* (2013, p. 3), 'schools are important contexts for the socialisation of young children's gender attitudes and behaviour' with increasing awareness that '[s]chool management and personnel embody a traditional gender value system which is constantly reinforced through the hidden curriculum' (Lynch and Feeley, 2009, p. 53).

This chapter begins with an overview of education in the Scottish context framed by a brief discussion of GIRFEC (*Getting It Right for Every Child*) (Scottish Government, 2012c) alongside the inclusive philosophies of the Curriculum for Excellence (CfE), and argues that both of these can be accessed to help children experiencing domestic abuse and more generally to frame preventative education principles. It goes

---

* The quotes from research participants in Chapter 6 are from Lombard, N. (2015) *Young People's Understandings of Men's Violence Against Women*, 1st edn, London: Routledge, and are reproduced with permission of the publishers.

on to examine how schools, and the broader education system, can often reinforce gender stereotypes through the 'hidden curriculum', which, in turn, sustains gender inequality and the dynamics underpinning domestic abuse. The chapter concludes with an examination of the integrated ways in which education is deployed in domestic abuse prevention work in Scottish schools.

The Scottish context: Education policy

Historically, Scotland has always maintained a separate education system to the rest of the UK (England, Wales and Northern Ireland) with its own legislation, governance and systems. Since devolution in 1999, education in Scotland has been the responsibility of the Scottish Parliament. National education and curricular policy is set by the Scottish government with parliamentary approval, while the implementation of national policy is the responsibility of Scotland's thirty-two local authority councils.

GIRFEC is the national approach in Scotland to improving outcomes and supporting the well-being of children and young people. As such, the GIRFEC framework is considered 'the bedrock for all children's services' (Scottish Government, 2012c, p. 5). It has strong educational implications, and is central to the aims of the CfE. A core principle of GIRFEC is to enable and empower children to reach their full potential using eight indicators, whereby children should be: safe; healthy; achieving; nurtured; active; respected; responsible; and included (SHANARRI). In practice, these indicators can help identify the impact of exposure to domestic abuse on individual children and highlight their specific support needs. Alongside working within the relevant policy frameworks, education professionals can practically support children experiencing domestic abuse in several ways. For example, a child may be given an Additional Support Plan (ASP) within school, to help with disrupted learning or to make staff aware of the wider issues particular pupils may be experiencing. In responding to the Scottish government's recommendations that: '[s]chools establish a nurturing ethos and culture which ensures that all young people including those with mental health difficulties to feel valued and engage with learning' (Scottish Government, 2016c, p. 29), nurture areas have been set up in some schools to support pupils who are living with violence at home (among other issues).

Stemming in part from a desire to encapsulate the overarching potential and transient nature of education, in 2010/11 Scotland introduced a national curriculum, the CfE, which aimed for transformational change in Scottish education (Scottish Government, 2008c). The curriculum covers ages 3–18, which includes pre-school, primary, secondary and post-secondary schooling. CfE has been lauded by educational experts the world over for its child-centred, non-prescriptive and progressive ethos. The Scottish government's position on education currently states:

> Children and young people's educational experience should open the doors to opportunities which enable children to become successful learners, confident individuals, responsible citizens and effective contributors to society (Scottish Government, 2017).

The CfE is universal and seeks to improve learner attainment, and also embodies a holistic, inclusive approach which recognises the need to offer more support to children from 'disadvantaged' backgrounds (Telfer, 2011, pp. 174–5). Those experiencing domestic abuse can certainly be included in this category, and the CfE aims to allow schools and teachers the flexibility to react to local needs and, specifically, the needs of each pupil (Priestley, 2013, p. 30).

Relationships, sexual health and parenthood education (RSHPE) is part of the Health and Well-being component of the CfE, and is intended to be delivered from the first year of primary school (P1) to the last year of secondary school (S6). Health and Well-being has the same importance, according to the Scottish government, as Literacy and Numeracy. Guidance on the Conduct of RSHPE in schools, produced by the Scottish government in 2014, emphasises the key role of trained, confident teachers in delivering good-quality RSHPE that meets the needs of pupils (Scottish Government, 2014b). The practicalities of the implementation of this approach are discussed below.

Education as a preventative strategy

Prevention is a core element of the Scottish government's strategy to address men's VAW. Prevention work has historically been carried out in two ways. Firstly, by raising awareness among the general public and wider communities. This is exemplified by the prolific Zero Tolerance poster campaign in the early 1990s (Mackay, 1996). Secondly, and of particular relevance to this chapter, it is implemented through primary prevention with the focus moving on to young people within educational settings.

The aims of educational prevention strategies are to increase awareness, change patterns of behaviour and develop the understanding that violence is wrong (Smaoun, 2000). Adopting a primary prevention approach challenges the notion that violence is inevitable and offers a vision about how things could be different. It aims to change societal attitudes, values and the structures that produce inequality. It raises fundamental questions about the way society is organised and can, as a result, be more challenging to individuals' core beliefs (Scottish Executive, 2003).

However, preventative work and educational awareness-raising have tended to take place with young people deemed 'old enough' to understand the implications of violence and abuse and judged likely to be in their own (sexual) relationships (Kelly *et al.*, 1991; Burton *et al.*, 1998; Holland *et al.*, 2004; Dublin Women's Aid, 1999; McCarry, 2003; Burman and Cartmel, 2005). Traditionally, children in primary schools or early years settings were rarely involved because they were seen as either in need of protection or too young to understand the complexities of adult relationships (Lombard, 2015), yet the necessity for an approach is highlighted below with the problematic perceptions that can exist in the early years.

The need for earlier prevention work that is framed by gender (in)equality

Research by Lombard (2013; 2014; 2015) examines what children and young people (aged 6–12) think about men's VAW with a view to informing both violence prevention and gender-equality work in this area. This research is drawn on here to highlight the problematic perceptions about domestic abuse held by young people and the need for preventative education that attends to gender roles. The research found that many primary school children normalised, naturalised and justified men's VAW, so this demonstrated the need for preventative work to start at a much earlier (st)age. It also found that, by critically reflecting on their own practice, teachers can have a positive influence on children's understanding of gender (adapted from recommendations by the Association of

Lecturers and Teachers, 2004; see also Lynch and Feeley, 2009; Barter and Lombard (2017) which in turn can lead children to challenge gender stereotypes and the limitations gender inequality perpetuates – including men's VAW.

The research also highlighted that children were more likely to label 'real' violence as between adult men (with visible injuries and official consequences) while violence occurring between young people was more likely to be termed 'unreal'. This not only results in girls being unable to access a framework by which to make sense of their own experiences (and boys' their own perpetration), but it also serves to invalidate and minimise many of their own experiences of violence and violent behaviour. This is often then replicated in their adult lives, where much behaviour is seen as what Dobash and Dobash (1992) termed the 'everyday interactions' between men and women.

Through the use of vignettes, children were encouraged to discuss their reactions to particular scenarios. One such vignette is illustrated below followed by how the participants (aged 11 and 12) made sense of the situation:

> Lizzy and Dave live in Glasgow. One day Lizzy goes out to the shops and when she comes back Dave asks her why dinner isn't ready? Lizzy says she has been busy and hasn't had the chance to make anything. Dave slaps Lizzy across the face and tells her that she shouldn't go to the shops without asking him first.

Young people would frequently frame their understanding of men's VAW as the result of women's lack of obedience, or not doing what they were told. The theme of obedience aligned women with domestic roles and duties:

> **Shazia**: But like what he should have done, what he should do next time is not slap her but say, next time dinner should be ready. I'm giving you your last warning. Because slapping her just makes things worser [sic].

Although Shazia maintains Dave should not have slapped Lizzy, she advocates that he uses the threat of violence to force her to obey him. Implicit in the notion of obedience is that of punishment and it is the man who has the power to request obedience and, therefore, generate the punishment. Some children expressed a belief that Lizzie should apologise for her 'behaviour', as well as Dave for his. This shows an agreement that Lizzie was wrong to go out without permission, to not get dinner ready on time and also that it was because of this 'failure' that Dave then hit her. He was not being violent, but simply seen as 'correcting' her. Therefore, it was his behaviour and not hers that was legitimated:

> **Paul**: Both of them should say that they are sorry. 'Cos she didn't ask to go out. She went out without his permission and he slapped her.
> **Iain**: Aye she should have told him.
> [...]
> **Michael**: She should at least contact him when she goes somewhere. He might be worried when she doesn't get back in time because his dinner wasn't ready.

Dave's reaction was justified as being a result of Lizzie failing to fulfil the expectations of her role as a woman. Connell (1987) argues that different organisations and institutions have gender regimes that interact or conflict with each other, generating a 'gender order'. The gender order changes over time, highlighting gender as transient and socially constructed, but maintained through both behaviour and practice. The gender order described by children in this study ranked differing forms of masculinity and femininity, with the most powerful and dominant at the top. This gender order unequivocally positions (heterosexual) men in a position of power, with the focus upon the woman's failing in her expected gender role.

This research highlights that, while children condone some forms of violence, perhaps more worryingly inequalities grounded in gender are still prevalent. In order to challenge and regenerate the gender order, teachers must respond with tangible actions that redress trends of gendered inequalities, the most pertinent of which is ending the separation of males and females into two homogenised groups. It is well-established that there are multiple masculinities and femininities (Connell and Messerschmidt, 2005; Lynch and Feeley, 2009, p. 57) and that the assignation of a binary separation is neither representative, constructive, worthwhile nor purposeful. The effects of doing so is limiting to individuals and reinforces hidden messages that there are characteristics or expectations associated with what it is to be either male or female.

Gender and educational inclusion

When learning about domestic abuse and challenging its roots, it is imperative that it is recognised as both a cause and consequence of male entitlement and privilege as well as of women's inequality. For this reason, any preventative education needs to be within the critical pedagogy model (Freire, 1996). Such a framework does not teach about the 'problem' (in this case domestic abuse) but rather examines the systems of power and structures of inequality that would enable 'learners' to understand why the problem exists in the first place. It is within this context that we argue that all violence prevention work should begin with gender equality education and training for educational practitioners.

The issue in education of gendered inequality, then, is not one of parity of involvement or direct discrimination. Rather, the 'hidden curriculum' indirectly excludes females from the benefits of education through: producing, reproducing and reinforcing ideals of gendered hegemony; influencing attitudes, subject choices and career paths; following a biased curriculum; and creating norms and gendered expectations around the use of space and resources. This is important because gender inequality underpins both men's violence and young people's understandings and constructions of it – so while we can work to prevent violence and the attitudes that help to perpetuate it, we cannot do so within current restrictive gender regimes that naturalise, normalise and justify men's violence. The fundamental shift that is needed in society's thinking is what Kelly (1999) terms a 'transformative equality' – that is challenging the structural, institutional and individual inequalities that enable gendered violence to persist.

The requirements to ensure equality, protection of rights, identity and to create the conditions for individual growth are set out in policy documents and associated legislation both at a devolved and UK-wide level –see, for example, GIRFEC (Scottish Government, 2012c); Equality Act 2010; Children and Young People's (Scotland) Act 2014; Education (Scotland) Act 2016. This ensures that schools are nurturing and encouraging children to find their own voice and their own identity – which extends to ensure children's interests and dispositions are protected while ensuring equality of opportunity. Furthermore, Scotland and the UK have ratified the UN Universal Declaration of Human Rights (UDHR, 1948) and the UN Convention on the Rights of the Child (UNCRC, 1989). This approach is also the foundation for understanding VAW by the Scottish government

(Scottish Government, 2014a). However, despite these requirements and the CfE, inequalities grounded in gender are still prevalent throughout education and the wider society both socially and structurally.

Successful violence prevention initiatives (in schools in Scotland)

In response to early research findings in the 1990s that showed older teenagers and young adults held worrying views about rape and consent (Burton *et al.*, 1998), the Zero Tolerance Charitable Trust developed and updated curricular materials for use in primary schools, secondary schools and informal youth settings. These aimed to empower young people with useful knowledge, skills and understanding and to promote positive, non-violent relationships based on equality and respect. While evaluations of the overall project were positive, the delivery of the work was viewed as patchy and inconsistent, with some teachers maintaining that their understanding of the issues had not improved and one-fifth viewing the programme as 'anti-male' (Reid Howie Associates, 2002, p. ii). Continued delivery of the programme was judged to be dependent upon (supportive) gatekeepers.

Further prevention work by Zero Tolerance, Rape Crisis Scotland and local education authorities has been delivered mainly in secondary schools, again with positive evaluations (see, for example, DMSS Research, 2015); however, delivery continues to be sporadic, usually because of resourcing issues and finances. In the last ten years , a number of initiatives aimed at older teenagers and university students have been used in Scotland. These programmes, such as Mentors in Violence Prevention (MVP), draw inspiration from US college campus bystander programmes, and have developed peer-delivered initiatives challenging young people to confront their own and others' role in perpetuating and sustaining GBV. MVP is run by the police together with secondary schools seeking to achieve attitudinal change. It is based upon the North American model devised by Jackson Katz (1995). Youth initiatives led the way before this. Through the Under Pressure programme (established 2011), for example, Zero Tolerance delivered training to professionals working with young people to increase their awareness of abuse in young people's relationships and to equip them with the skills to address it (see Zero Tolerance and YWCA Scotland, 2011). Other initiatives have included drama and theatre performances or short films with workbook activities. The National Children and Young People's Prevention Network (NCYPPN) and Baldy Bane Theatre Company created *Crush* and *Gold Stars & Dragon Marks* with input from children and young people including those affected by domestic abuse. While Stanley *et al.* (2015, p. xxi) in their PEACH (preventing domestic abuse for children) review praised the approach taken by such drama-based initiatives, they also warned of the limitations of one-off, stand-alone performances for generating sustained attitudinal change.

It is critical that external agencies should not replace delivery of appropriate programmes by teachers, but rather their input should be complementary. Difficulties arise when additional programmes are not embedded across a school, not delivered within a supportive ethos, or when they are delivered as stand-alone programmes.

RSHPE does not receive as much time in the school curriculum as many young people and teachers would like (Healthy Respect, 2016). It is often 'squeezed out' by examinable subjects or those studies leading to an award or qualification. This, sometimes haphazard, approach to prevention education coupled with the dearth in funding is unfortunately a UK-wide problem highlighted in the PEACH study by Stanley *et al.* (2015, p. xxi) who advised that:

> Longer interventions delivered by trained staff appear more effective. Teachers are well placed to embed interventions in schools but they require training and support from those with specialist domestic abuse knowledge.

The piecemeal approach to intervention was also identified as a major problem by Rape Crisis Scotland and Zero Tolerance in their ongoing development of the 'whole school approach' (discussed below). Currently, in Scotland, the learning experience of young people is dependent upon local authority provision, expertise within the school and sometimes the involvement of external organisations whether they are statutory, such as the police (MVP), or voluntary (Rape Crisis Scotland). Adopting a 'whole school approach' takes a holistic approach to GBV prevention, with measures addressing school ethos, policy, staff capacity and capability, young people's participation, curriculum and safeguarding (see DMSS Research, 2015). Such an approach is embedded within schools rather than simply 'added on'. Current initiatives in primary schools (Barter and Lombard,

2017) and those proposed by *Equally Safe* (Scottish Government, 2014a) place gender equality at the centre of prevention and education work in both primary and secondary schools, building upon the requirement for RSHPE as part of Health and Well-being in the CfE.

What more can schools do?

All schools have the potential to make a key contribution to preventative education in their roles as institutions reaching thousands of young people daily. However, schools can also be sites of inequality and harmful behaviour (Manjoo and Nadj, 2015). The recent report by the UK Government Women and Equalities Committee (2016) drew attention to high levels of sexual harassment and GBV in schools, noting the possible impact on educational attainment as well as the potential harm to future relationships and health, as had been noted by other work in North America (e.g. Stein, 1995). It recommended that sexual harassment and violence are tackled via a 'whole school approach', where the issues are embedded and tackled in the day-to-day running of schools, holistically, rather than simply being treated as an isolated lesson (UK Government Women and Equalities Committee, 2016). Acker (1990) states that, to address inequalities, the structure and interactions of an institution must be addressed – and it is this we would argue that can provide the foundations for a 'whole school approach', as has been adopted by the Welsh government (Welsh Government, 2015 see also Humphreys *et al.*, 2008).

Protecting the identity and characteristics of children while ensuring recognition and equality is both a professional and legal requirement as well as a morally important one, grounded in humanity (see Freire, 1996). On that basis, teachers are required to ensure that their practice does not limit the experiences and opportunities of individuals on grounds of gender and that they embrace a 'whole school approach' to challenging inequality and violence. In doing this, schools can identify and denounce abuse when it happens in schools, among pupils and to teachers. By embedding and promoting a 'whole school approach', a safe and equal learning environment can be provided that benefits and protects all.

As an institution, education can address gender inequality by, for example, not reinforcing gender divisions by placing male teachers with older children or by assuming females are more suited to roles associated with infants. Teachers can reflect on the division of jobs distributed to children in the classroom and not give heavier/more physically demanding jobs (e.g. shifting tables) to boys and 'softer' jobs (e.g. tidying away crayons) to girls. Teachers should ensure that physical spaces are not divided by gender (e.g. cloakrooms) and need to be conscientious about ensuring girls have equal access to all spaces and resources. Teachers should be aware of limiting symbols that they may use, and curricular content should be adapted as far as possible to ensure that gender bias is eliminated. Teachers should be prepared to consistently challenge gender stereotypes and promote positive gender roles while addressing preconceptions that children may have about what boys and girls can and cannot do. This list is not exhaustive but serves as a summary of just some of the actions that teachers can take to counter the 'hidden curriculum'.

Conclusion

This chapter has made clear that, when it comes to preventing violence (including domestic abuse), early intervention is key. Schools, therefore, are an ideal setting for providing this foundation through challenging the gender inequality that underpins the violence and also by leading the way in attitudinal change through the promotion of healthy, respectful relationships. However, as several initiatives have shown, it is not always easy to engineer such change and many of the obstacles come down to time and money as well as the supportive environments of the individual schools. We argue that the inclusive curriculum offered by the CfE provides fertile ground for the development of an innovative (RSHPE) programme. The sustained promotion of gender equality through teacher training and in day-to-day practice is a necessary framework in which the Scottish government's *Equally Safe* (Scottish Government, 2014a) preventative agenda can be encouraged to flourish.

Embedding a 'whole school approach' to challenging inequality and violence offers a potentially fruitful way of ensuring a safe and equal learning environment that benefits and protects all. More importantly, all education programmes and awareness training need to be underpinned by solid understandings of gender and gender (in)equality. Fully informed, properly trained and committed teachers are key. Teachers in Scotland can encourage the promotion of positive, respectful relationships and the prevention of violence through sustained delivery of the CfE. This is particularly the case in relation to the promotion of messages around healthy relationships, issues of control and, drawing on the WHO (2006) definition of sexual well-being, respecting the sexual rights of others. Young people's personal narratives can challenge restrictive forms of gender; this needs to be supported and encouraged within and throughout the educational process. Building upon this concern with the experiences of children and young people, in the following chapter Morrison and Mitchell highlight the considerable impact of domestic abuse on children and the role of social work services in protecting them from these harms.

CHAPTER 7

Domestic Abuse and the Role of Children and Families' Social Work

Fiona Morrison and Anna Mitchell

Introduction

In this chapter, we explore the role that children and families' social work plays in identifying and responding to the needs of children with experience of domestic abuse. We use the phrase 'children and families' social work' to refer to statutory services provided by local authorities in Scotland. These are services that the Social Work (Scotland) Act 1968 and the Children (Scotland) Act 1995 require local authorities to provide to safeguard and promote the welfare of children who are in need.

The chapter begins with an overview of the literature on children and domestic abuse, making the case why children's experiences of domestic abuse are important and salient issues for children and families' social work. The chapter then explores children and families' social work response to domestic abuse. We highlight how Scottish child welfare legislation has shifted the way in which domestic abuse is conceptualised in this context. We also discuss the research on the response to domestic abuse in a children and families' social work context, exploring the tensions and dilemmas in this area of practice. In the final part of this chapter, we turn to innovative developments currently underway in Scottish children and families' social work practice in relation to domestic abuse. Here we focus on how one local authority – the City of Edinburgh Council – has embarked upon a process of change that aims to transform the ways that social workers respond to and deal with children, adult victims and perpetrators of domestic abuse. In discussing the Safe and Together Model, we explore the potential for children and families' social work to make more visible and address the harmful impacts that domestic abuse can have on children's lives.

Children and domestic abuse

Since the 1990s, there has been a rapid growth in research about children and domestic abuse. This body of knowledge has enhanced our understanding of children and domestic abuse in two fundamental ways. Firstly, it has underlined the scale of the problem. Secondly, it has cast light on the intimate ways that domestic abuse affects and constrains children's lives. This section explores both of these areas, making the case why domestic abuse is an important issue for those working in children and families' social work.

The scale and impact of domestic abuse

Studies about prevalence underline that domestic abuse is an issue for many children. Murray (2016) provides analysis on partner abuse data collected as part of the 2014/15 SCJS (see Scottish Government, 2016d). She reports that 39.4% of those who experienced partner abuse in the last twelve months had children who were living in the same household when the most recent incident took place (Murray, 2016, pp. 38–9). Of these cases, almost two-thirds involved children being either present or close by when the incident took place. It is important to acknowledge that a significant limitation of crime surveys such as the SCJS is that they tend not to involve children and instead rely upon adults' reporting of children's experiences (see Devaney, 2015). The UK-wide prevalence study on abuse carried out by the National Society for the Prevention of Cruelty to Children (NSPCC) is, therefore, useful here in exploring the scale of children's experiences of domestic abuse. Carried out with children and young adults, this research found 12% of under eleven year olds, 17.5% of 11–17 year olds and 23.7% of 18–24 year olds had been exposed to domestic violence between adults in their homes during childhood (Radford *et al.*, 2011, p. 47).

A number of studies have suggested that witnessing violence towards their mother constitutes emotional or psychological abuse of children (e.g. Jaffe *et al.*, 1990; McGee, 2000). This is supported by research showing that children living with domestic abuse exhibit higher rates of depression and anxiety (e.g. Buckley *et al.*, 2007), are more likely to have symptoms associated with trauma (Hornor, 2005; Levendosky *et al.*, 2002) and have significantly more behavioural and emotional problems when compared with children who do not live with domestic violence (Meltzer *et al.*, 2009).

Research also shows that there is a close connection between domestic abuse and the direct abuse of children, and this can make the distinction between the categories of domestic abuse and child abuse difficult. The NSPCC prevalence study found that young people living with family violence were between three and four times more likely to experience physical violence and neglect than other children who did not live with family violence (Radford *et al.*, 2011). Stanley (2011), Devaney (2015) and Holt *et al.* (2008) all provide thorough international overviews of evidence on the impact domestic abuse has on children, highlighting the associations between domestic abuse and short- and long-term outcomes for children. However, it is important to stress that the evidence on the links between domestic abuse and outcomes for children is inconclusive. There is conflicting evidence about whether the effects on boys and girls are different (e.g. Evans *et al.*, 2008; Wolfe *et al.*, 2003) or whether age can ameliorate or worsen the impact on children (e.g. Wolfe *et al.*, 2003). Uncertainty about the impact of domestic abuse on children is further compounded when we consider Kitzmann *et al.*'s (2003) meta-analysis of 118 research studies. They found children with experience of domestic violence to have significantly poorer outcomes for twenty-one developmental and behavioural dimensions than other children. However, they also report one-third of children exposed to domestic violence do not appear to do any worse than other children.

The ways in which children's lives are affected

How we understand children's experiences of domestic abuse has been transformed by research carried out with children themselves about their own perspectives and accounts of domestic abuse. McGee's (2000) and Mullender *et al.*'s (2002) research are two early and important examples of this. It has made clear that children are rarely protected from the knowledge that domestic abuse is occurring in their family; indeed, they are affected by domestic abuse and by no means passive in it.

So, in what ways are children affected by domestic abuse? In combining Holden (2003) and McGee's (1997) work, Stanley (2011, p. 29) provides a useful framework that helps us understand the key ways that children experience and are affected by domestic abuse:

- before birth (there is growing recognition of the heightened risk of domestic abuse during pregnancy – see Chapter 5 on approaches to addressing this in health settings);
- witnessing domestic abuse directly or indirectly (e.g. being physically present when the abuse takes place or overhearing abuse);
- being directly abused;
- dealing with the aftermath of abuse (e.g. parental injury or parental separation);
- participation in the abuse of their mother.

Children describe living with domestic abuse as existing in a climate of fear (Mullender *et al.*, 2002; Katz, 2015), where home life and the relationships in it are precarious and often undermined (Mullender *et al.*, 2002; Laing *et al.*, 2013; Katz, 2015). Children describe feelings of shame and stigma associated with their experience of domestic abuse, which can lead to withdrawal from peer activities and friendships (McGee, 2000; Gorin, 2004), and may make it difficult for children to seek help (Buckley *et al.*, 2006).

Research also shows that children experience severe disruptions to their lives as a result of domestic abuse. Stafford *et al.*'s (2007) Scottish qualitative study with thirty children found examples where children have had to move home up to eight times during a period of two years to flee from the perpetrator of domestic abuse. These repeated upheavals to children and young people's lives are characterised by disruptions to their education, loss of friends, family members and possessions. Children reported resentment about 'missing out' on their childhood. They gave examples of having to look after or protect younger siblings, where they were compelled to keep domestic abuse a secret, where they lived with constant fear and intimidation, and where they felt responsible for ending the violence (e.g. Mullender *et al.*, 2002). Research also shows how children take action in these difficult circumstances. They develop their own coping strategies (Mullender *et al.*, 2002; Stafford *et al.*, 2007; Øverlien and Hydén, 2009), they take a stand against it (Øverlien and Hydén, 2009) and act in ways to promote their, and their mothers', recovery (Mullender *et al.*, 2002; Katz, 2015).

There are two final and important messages from research about children and domestic abuse; both relate to how domestic abuse is conceptualised. Firstly, as was discussed in Chapters 2, 3 and 4, the passage of the

Domestic Abuse (Scotland) Act 2018, influenced by the work of Stark (2007), has clear implications for how we consider children's experiences of domestic abuse. It means that our gaze must broaden, beyond incidents of violence to consider how sustained psychological abuse affects adult and, indeed, child victims. Secondly, there has been a tendency in policy and practice to assume that the ending of a relationship translates with the ending of domestic abuse. Research shows this is often not the case as domestic abuse may continue and escalate following separation, and children's post-separation contact with fathers may provide opportunities for abuse to continue (e.g. Holt, 2015; Thiara and Gill, 2012; Radford and Hester, 2006). Morrison's (2014) Scottish qualitative research elaborates on this. The study involved eighteen children aged 8–14 and sixteen mothers who had experienced domestic abuse in Scotland. It found that, even with legal protective measures such as interdicts in place, domestic abuse continued and that children's contact and relationships with fathers became a focal point for this. The research also underlined the significance that emotional abuse has in post-separation parenting arrangements, the fear it engenders and the distress it causes to both adult and child victims. This broadens our understanding of the ways in which children's lives are affected by domestic abuse. It highlights that the effects of domestic abuse can be far-reaching and may continue even when children no longer live with the perpetrator of abuse.

A social work response to domestic abuse

The growing body of knowledge about children and domestic abuse has paved the way for domestic abuse to be seen an issue of child welfare and, in turn, a concern for children and families' social work. Across jurisdictions, we can see this shift through changes in policy and legislation that increasingly regard domestic abuse as an issue for child protection. This may also be observed in Scottish child welfare legislation. The Children's Hearings System is the care and justice system for children and young people in Scotland. It aims to ensure the safety and well-being of vulnerable children and young people through a decision-making lay tribunal called the Children's Panel. The Children's Hearings (Scotland) Act 2011 amended the Children (Scotland) Act 1995 to include new and specific grounds for children's referral to the Children's Hearings System because of domestic abuse:

Section 67(f) The child has, or is likely to have, a close connection with a person who has carried out domestic abuse.

The circumstances in which a child is defined as having a close connection with a person is set out in section 67:

Section 67(3) (a) The child is a member of the same household as the person, or (b) the child is not a member of the same household as the person but the child has significant contact with the person.

Morrison *et al.* (2013) carried out research about child contact and domestic abuse, part of which examined professionals' views about potential implications of these new grounds for referral. These included: that the legislation had potential to make domestic abuse more visible; conflicting views about whether this would increase the numbers of referrals made to the Children's Hearings System about domestic abuse; a concern whether this might increase litigation among parents; and that the legislation created more appropriate grounds for referral. The last point warrants further explanation. Previously referrals made about domestic abuse to the Children's Reporter came under section 52(2)(c) of the Children (Scotland) Act 1995. This categorisation of domestic abuse as a 'lack of parental care' was seen as inappropriate. Often it meant that the focus was on the non-abusing parent (in most cases the mother), rather than the parent or other adult who was carrying out the abuse. These new grounds were seen to have the potential to positively shift the focus of Children's Panels towards the person responsible for carrying out domestic abuse – an issue we will return to again in this chapter.

A child protection response to domestic abuse

While greater recognition of the impact of domestic abuse on children may be welcome, constructing domestic abuse as an issue for child protection is problematic. The scale of domestic abuse means that it has the potential to draw significant numbers of children and families into social work services (Morrison *et al.*, 2013; Stanley *et al.*, 2011). This highlights a very real concern about the capacity of social work to deal with domestic abuse. Reflecting on the English experience, Peckover (2014) notes that, while policy developments have led professionals to become more aware of those affected by domestic abuse, a focus on identification (e.g. police notifications to social services or automatic referrals to the Children's Reporter in a Scottish context) has not necessarily translated to improved safety or support for women and children. This is exemplified in Stanley *et al.*'s (2011) English research on police notifications, where the majority of children referred to social services because of domestic violence did not meet the threshold for statutory intervention. This, alongside a dearth of non-statutory support services, meant that the majority of children, despite now being known to social work, continued to live with domestic abuse without support or intervention. As Humphreys and Bradbury-Jones (2015, p. 232) argue, there needs to be a: 'differentiat[ed] response ... to ensure that only children and families that reach the threshold for a tertiary statutory response should be referred or notified'. To be clear, this does not mean that children who experience domestic abuse do not need support or help; however, it does mean that a social work or child protection response may not be appropriate for all children who experience domestic abuse. A further caveat comes from Devaney (2008) and Cleaver *et al.* (2007), who note that often when domestic abuse is present so too are a range of other social problems, such as drug or alcohol misuse or poor mental health. When children are living with multiple adversities, responses must take account of all these complex issues (Humphreys and Bradbury-Jones, 2015).

Tensions in social work practice

In cases of domestic abuse, social workers have the difficult task of identifying and balancing the connected but, at times, competing needs of children, the non-abusing adult and the adult who is the perpetrator of domestic abuse. In this context, it can be difficult to ascertain what the focus of the social work intervention ought to be and to maintain this focus (Peckover and Trotter, 2015). Laing *et al.* (2013) explore the international evidence about social work responses to domestic abuse. They report on common themes from across the evidence base and point to how practice in this area may usefully develop, including the following areas.

Challenging the 'failure to protect' narrative

This relates to a tendency in practice to hold mothers living with domestic abuse responsible for protecting their children, rather than the perpetrator of abuse. Instead of placing unrealistic expectations such as leaving the relationship or having sole responsibility for protecting children, practice should shift towards supporting mothers and providing advocacy for them (Radford and Hester, 2006).

Engaging with and making the perpetrator visible

Women rather than men have been the enduring focus of social work (Waterhouse and McGhee, 2015). While not all perpetrators of abuse are men, there is real concern that an exclusive focus on mothers renders the perpetrator of domestic abuse invisible, even though their behaviour continues to pose a risk to children and women.

Seeing and addressing both the child and adult victims' needs

By its very nature, domestic abuse has both child and adult victims; a response must, therefore, see and take account of both. A key challenge for statutory social work is that it is not established, organised or resourced to respond to adult victimisation. Laing *et al.* (2013) further argue that a forensic child protection approach that has investigating and substantiating abuse as its principal focus means that support to address children and adult victims' needs is often missing in practice.

Changing children and families' social work practice: Developing the 'Safe and Together Model' at the City of Edinburgh Council

Having examined the challenges and tensions in a child protection response to domestic abuse and in social work practice, we now turn to new and promising developments in Scotland that aim to address some of these issues. A recent advancement in children and families' social work practice in relation to domestic abuse is the development of the Safe and Together Model by David Mandel (2014). Originating from the US, it has since been adopted in a few states in Australia and in parts of Scotland. The City of Edinburgh Council is one local authority in Scotland that has recently begun work to embed the Safe and Together Model across all agencies that work with children affected by domestic abuse.

In 2014, the City of Edinburgh Council undertook an audit of child protection cases where domestic abuse was an issue (City of Edinburgh Council, 2018). The audit focused on cases from across the city where there had been three or more police callouts during a six-month period and subsequently a children and families' social worker had undertaken a risk and needs assessment of the child(ren) concerned. A total of twenty-six cases were analysed, and the following themes about responses to domestic abuse were identified:

- an overemphasis on singular incidents of physical violence, rather than recognition of a wider pattern of abuse and control;
- the assumption that separation or removal of the perpetrator will automatically reduce risk;
- the placing of responsibility for care of the children and for ending the abuse primarily with the victim, while superficially engaging with perpetrators;
- the explicit encouragement of separation, without addressing risks around safe contact or ongoing disruption to family life.

As discussed earlier, these are familiar issues for social work practice and it is these that the Safe and Together Model aims to address. After the 2014 audit, Edinburgh's Child Protection Committee agreed to support training for practitioners on the Safe and Together Model. Following training, practitioners became 'champions' for the Safe and Together Model, acting to raise awareness of the model and develop the practice of their colleagues.

Safe and Together is a practice model that aims to improve how child welfare systems and practitioners respond to the issue of domestic abuse. It provides a common framework for practitioners to consider and discuss concerns, challenges and solutions for families experiencing domestic abuse. Three key principles underpin the model: (i) being child centred; (ii) working in a strengths-based way with non-abusing parents; and (iii) focusing on the perpetrator's behaviour (Mandel, 2014). These three principles underpin the Safe and Together Model and are used to guide assessment and case decisions. We now elaborate on these principles and discuss the potential they have to improve responses to domestic abuse.

Principles underpinning the Safe and Together Model
Keeping the child safe and together with the non-abusing parent
The first principle is that, when professionals engage with families affected by domestic abuse, they should aim to keep the child safe and together with the non-abusing parent. This comes from the understanding that this is usually the most effective way to promote children's safety, healing from trauma, stability and nurturance.

Strengths-based approach with non-abusing parent
The second principle states that professionals should endeavour to develop a strengths-based partnership with non-abusing parents. This approach is likely to be the most efficient and child-centred way of assessing risk through mutual information sharing.

Focusing on the perpetrators of domestic abuse
The third principle states that professionals should aim to intervene with the perpetrator to reduce risk and harm to the child. Engaging with perpetrators and holding them accountable in a variety of ways, including court processes, reduces the risks to children. For example, the City of Edinburgh Council's case file audit found that many actions within the child's plan relating to domestic abuse rested with the victim. The Safe and Together Model encourages social workers to take behaviourally focused actions within children's plans so that the perpetrator can be made visible, held accountable for their abuse and that changes in their behaviour can be monitored.

Critical components of Safe and Together Model
A well as key principles, there are also critical components of the Safe and Together Model. These components aim to support practical and tangible changes to practice with families affected by domestic abuse. They support practitioners to consider domestic abuse more fully in their information gathering, case planning, safety planning, assessment and the role of other adversities in children's lives. The critical components of the Safe and Together Model are the following.

The perpetrator's pattern of coercive control

The first component asks professionals to outline the perpetrator's pattern of coercive control. It aims to identify all forms of abuse and control in both current and previous relationships, rather than outline singular incidents of physical abuse. Information about the perpetrator's pattern of abuse in both previous and current relationships can be found in criminal background checks, files and case notes of all family members and in wider discussions with the clients, their family, friends and other professionals. The City of Edinburgh Council's case file audit found that, within case files, there was rich information about the perpetrator's pattern of abuse which was not easily visible and, at times, was not reflected in assessments or reports. The model encourages fact-based, behaviourally focused descriptions within assessments and reports so that the pattern of abuse and control is clear.

Actions taken by the perpetrator to harm the child

The second component asks professionals to outline how actions taken by the perpetrator have harmed the child. This includes describing direct physical, emotional and sexual abuse of the child. It also involves exploring how domestic abuse has harmed the child: for example, what the child may have seen or heard; where they were when the abuse took place; or how the perpetrator may have treated them before, during and after the incident.

Non-abusing parent's protective efforts

The third component explores the full spectrum of the non-abusing parent's efforts to promote the safety and well-being of the child. The City of Edinburgh Council's case file audit showed that separation, moving home or calling the police were viewed as the primary routes of safety for children, and that responsibility for carrying out these plans usually rested with the non-abusing parent. While these may provide safety in some cases, there can be a 'one size fits all' approach to case planning, which becomes the definition of what constitutes a 'protective parent'. It also risks not recognising the nuanced and multiple ways that non-abusing parents protect their children. Non-abusing parents are parenting in adverse circumstances, but may still display protective efforts such as: maintaining medical appointments or feeding and educational routines; ensuring children have extra-curricular activities or contact with friends and family; talking with their children about domestic abuse and developing safety plans; physically protecting their children or encouraging them to leave during an attack; or modifying their own behaviour in an attempt to reduce abuse and their children's exposure to it.

Adverse impact of the perpetrator's behaviour on the child

The impact of the perpetrator's pattern of abuse is outlined using the fourth component. However, rather than primarily focusing on the direct impact on the child – whether the child saw the abuse, heard it, were being held or were directly involved – it aims to describe the wide-ranging impact that the perpetrator's behaviour has on the child. Consideration is given as to how the abuse adversely impacts on all aspects of well-being: for example, describing the impact of numerous house and school moves; loss of contact with family or friends; or loss of income and stability.

The role of other adversities

Finally, the role of substance abuse, mental health, culture and other socio-economic factors is examined in the fifth component. This supports professionals to consider issues such as substance misuse and mental health through the lens of the domestic abuse: for example, by considering how domestic abuse may cause or exacerbate the non-abusing parent's substance misuse or prevent them from healing by interfering in their efforts to access support. It also helps to clarify that the perpetrator's substance misuse and mental health problems are not the cause of the domestic abuse, but may relate to their pattern of abuse in complex ways.

The original City of Edinburgh Council audit on social work practice, which was completed in 2014, was repeated in 2017. It found qualitative changes to practice in assessment and planning since the introduction of the Safe and Together Model. This included: greater attempts made by social workers to explore patterns of coercive control both current and historic; greater attention in case files given to the non-abusing parent's protective parenting; an increased recognition of the wide-ranging impact of domestic abuse on the child; and increased clarity of what parents are expected to do to improve outcomes for children (City of Edinburgh Council, 2018).

Conclusion

This chapter has established why domestic abuse is an important issue for children and families' social work and has explored the role that children and families' social work plays in responding to the needs of children with experience of domestic abuse. The dilemmas that arise from conceptualising domestic abuse as a child protection issue, which includes support for children who do not meet the threshold for a statutory intervention as well as the need for a differentiated response to children affected by domestic abuse, have been discussed.

The Safe and Together Model appears to be a promising approach in supporting children and families' social workers in their response to domestic abuse. Looking forward, it is important that this work is evaluated. There is a need to examine the short- and long-term outcomes for children, non-abusing adults and perpetrators. Key to this are the perspectives of the children, non-abusing parents and perpetrators who experience this model, as are the perspectives of the social workers who are tasked with implementing it. Also important is that there are adequate resources to address the longer-term therapeutic and support needs of this group of children and non-abusing parents. Likewise, the needs of the many more children who experience domestic abuse, but do not meet the threshold for statutory intervention, must not be forgotten.

CHAPTER 8:

Conclusion: Looking back, moving forward ('Ahin/gang forward')

Clare McFeely, Michele Burman and Oona Brooks-Hay

Introduction

Scotland's approach to domestic abuse is recognised as world leading. Following sustained lobbying by the women's movement in Scotland, from the late 1990s onwards, the Scottish government and the statutory sector have taken increasing responsibility for understanding, preventing and responding to domestic abuse. This has led to a ground-breaking policy definition, greater awareness of the 'harms' of domestic abuse, a more nuanced understanding of its complex and multifaceted nature and the introduction of a raft of policy and legislative reform across sectors. Given the multidimensional nature of domestic abuse and the multiple consequences that it generates, the implementation of preventative and response measures involves different actors and agencies. It demands a corresponding multidimensional approach, integrating legislative and preventative action, protection of victim–survivors and support services covering different areas of intervention, as well as prosecution and treatment of perpetrators. Responsibility cuts across (local and national) government sectors including criminal justice, healthcare, education, social services and employment (Burman and Johnstone, 2015).

This book considers the key innovations in research, policy, legislation and practice, which have aimed to address domestic abuse and its nefarious effects. At the same time, it highlights the pervasiveness of domestic abuse in women's lives and the challenges that it continues to pose for policymakers and practitioners working to develop effective ways of preventing, recognising and responding to domestic abuse. While the examples explored in the book are, for the most part,

specific to Scotland, the challenges discussed are international concerns: for example, ongoing debates about definition, including the
focus on coercive and controlling behaviour; the increased volume of
domestic abuse cases coming to attention; the adequacy and sustain-
ability of service provision; and the viability of partnership working.
With these challenges in mind, in this chapter we reflect on the progress
made in Scotland to date, consider some of the persistent challenges
in tackling domestic abuse, and highlight more current initiatives. Key
themes emerging from the preceding chapters are discussed in relation
to the book's underpinning focus on conceptualising, responding to and
preventing domestic abuse. It is argued that, while domestic abuse is
undoubtedly a prevalent and persistent problem, it is not inevitable and
that 'a different world is possible' (EVAW, 2011).

Conceptualising domestic abuse

In Chapter 1, it is argued that the way in which domestic abuse is conceptualised is fundamental to how it is measured, understood and
responded to. Yet this remains a contentious issue both nationally and
internationally. The identification of domestic abuse and other forms of
GBV as a cause and consequence of gender inequality is the cornerstone
of Scotland's gendered approach. This gendered analysis of domestic
abuse, which originated in grass-roots organisations in Scotland, was
rapidly adopted by national government and implemented across a
range of policy areas (Scottish Executive, 2001), though it was not, at
that time, shared by other parts of the UK. This gendered understanding
underpins activity across a range of organisations that respond to those
affected by domestic abuse. Along with an increased understanding of
the nature of domestic abuse has come an acknowledgement of coercive
and controlling behaviour as a cumulative form of subjugation (Stark,
2007), which emphasises the controlling impacts of behaviour rather
than individual acts.

Awareness of the complex nature of domestic abuse among practitioners and policymakers has developed considerably in recent years, yet satisfactory measurement of this abuse remains at something of an impasse
within Scotland – and the UK more broadly (Myhill, 2017). This is, in
no small part, due to the challenges inherent in attempting to measure an
ongoing pattern of behaviour and diversity in the perpetration and experience of domestic abuse. If improvements in understanding and measuring
domestic abuse are to be made, it is imperative that researchers, practition-

ers and policymakers have shared theoretical and conceptual frameworks that assist collation and interpretation of research in this area.

Going forward, technological developments, which offer opportunities to reach and support women experiencing abuse and to promote wider cultural change, also have evolving implications for controlling and coercive behaviour. Social networking and smart technology represent new ways in which women's behaviour can be monitored and controlled via mobile phones, email accounts and social networking sites. Hence as the shape and form of domestic abuse evolves over time, agencies need to be both attentive and equipped to address the new challenges that these developments will undoubtedly present.

Responding to Domestic Abuse
Mainstream or specialised provision?
A growing recognition of the nature of domestic abuse, the context in which it occurs and its impact on those exposed to it has resulted in the development of expert practitioners, primarily from within the third sector but also the inception of specialist teams within statutory agencies. This is particularly evident in the growth of dedicated roles to meet the specific demands of policing and prosecuting domestic abuse, discussed in Chapters 3 and 4. Yet, contributors to this book have identified that women and children exposed to domestic abuse are seeking support and, to some extent, are receiving a response from mainstream, non-specialist services (e.g. housing, health, education and social work agencies). The far-reaching impact and extent of domestic abuse is such that reliance on specialised teams alone is not feasible. Furthermore, the breadth of support requirements necessitates a coordinated multi-agency response.

Scotland's current strategy for preventing and responding to violence against women and girls, *Equally Safe* (Scottish Government, 2016a), states that responding to domestic abuse is 'everyone's responsibility'. In addition, statutory sector workers also have a duty to identify and protect those affected by domestic abuse. Therefore, this work should be recognised as 'core' work for these organisations. In some areas, this is already explicit, such as children and families' social work services, discussed in Chapter 7 by Morrison and Mitchell. In health, training is delivered to registered health professionals in priority areas, but, more recently, this training has been incorporated into the pre-registration education at some universities, thus increasing awareness and skills of all nurses (and in some areas of doctors and dentists) on their duty to respond to suspicion or disclosure of domestic abuse. In Chapter 6, Lombard and Harris recommended that a similar approach could be beneficial in education through the introduction of gender equality to teacher training.

Access to support and services from health, social care, education and the police is negotiated between those who experience domestic abuse and individual practitioners (albeit within the constraints of overarching protocols). Therefore, the beliefs and attitudes of practitioners influence the degree to which services are sensitive, attuned to the inherent gendered dynamics, and responsive to the needs of women and children affected by domestic abuse. As such, the approach of individual practitioners cannot be underestimated. In Chapter 5, McFeely and Cosgrove highlighted progress on this issue with regard to health practitioners. The systematic approach to address the medicalisation of abuse, implemented by NHS Scotland, has positively altered organisational perceptions of domestic abuse. This presents some grounds for optimism, as well as a practical approach to supporting change within organisational culture. Yet, a considerable challenge remains in monitoring practice and supporting changes at an individual level in order to sustain meaningful organisational transformation. This challenge presents across a number of sectors. As noted in Chapters 3 and 4, in order for the reforms within criminal justice that are intended to improve the experiences of victims to be realised, then the responses of criminal justice personnel are key. As such, it is crucial that they understand the complex nature of abusive behaviour, including the centrality of gender dynamics (Hester, 2011).

Creation of a new bespoke offence of domestic abuse

As discussed in Chapters 2 and 4, Scotland's recent creation of a new specific offence of domestic abuse represents one of the most radical attempts yet to align the criminal justice response with contemporary policy and feminist conceptual understandings of domestic abuse as a form of coercive control (Burman and Brooks-Hay, 2018). Quite how this will play out is as yet unknown. While legislation has been introduced criminalising 'coercive and controlling behaviour' in England and Wales, the evidence base about its operationalisation and usage is underdeveloped, largely because of the limited time elapsed since its introduction. Going forward, significant challenges are anticipated for the new offence, not least that there are very likely to be some difficulties around the identification and recognition of some forms of coercive and controlling behaviour, unless women are supported to come forward to articulate it and the police are fully equipped to recognise it as domestic abuse. Ongoing training of criminal justice professionals is key in this regard. Even where police are responding appropriately under the terms of the new offence, there are likely to be challenges in corroborating a 'course of conduct' of abusive behaviour, as well as corroborating emotional and psychological abuse, because of its inherently private nature. Guarding against the secondary victimisation of victim–survivors through likely requirements for supplementary evidence to substantiate facts will require vigilance from the court.

Multi-agency collaboration

Much of the work addressing domestic abuse in Scotland takes place on a multi-agency basis. With national government positioning domestic abuse as a priority and providing a strategic lead, Scotland's decentralisation both empowers local authorities and renders them accountable for identifying and responding to priority needs. While the nature of arrangements varies, there are domestic abuse partnerships and/or training consortia in all local authority areas in Scotland, generally composed of statutory (police; housing; social work; community services; local NHS Boards) and third-sector organisations.

The work of the feminist movement in Scotland in shaping the current approach and policy landscape is recognised in Chapter 1. A strong feminist voice remains to this day through third-sector organisations, and also resonates through the approach of decision makers within statutory agencies. The role of the third sector is crucial; as Robinson and Hudson (2011) argue, the third sector can be perceived as a more approachable and palatable option for support-seeking than statutory organisations for women who have had negative experiences of a service response in the past. Third-sector organisations continue to collaborate and often take a lead in progressing policies and translating them to practice, as recognised in *Equally Safe*:

There is a wealth of knowledge and experience across Scotland
and beyond for us to tap into and build upon, much of which
has been developed by our partners in the third sector from
many years and decades of working directly with women and
children who have experienced violence and abuse (Scottish
Government, 2016a, p. 54).

Nonetheless, challenges in partnership working exist between and
within sectors. Insular practice models can present a challenge as professions with different agendas and potentially conflicting perspectives are
required to work together. Hester (2004) describes organisations functioning in separate spheres with fundamentally incompatible perspectives as a
product of services developing their own analysis and response independently over time. Hence, despite a clear national definition and analysis
of domestic abuse, areas of divergence may persist in respect of who and
how to protect. While Scottish multi-agency experience is not without ten-
sion in some areas, the local multi-agency consortia and the policy focus
on close working and greater sharing of information combine to alleviate
barriers to engagement wherever possible.

Sustainability of service provision
While responding to domestic abuse is core business for all statutory sectors, this is supported by specialist third-sector organisations through
provision of direct support to survivors of abuse as well as by advice and
information to colleagues within the statutory organisations. In order
for specialist third-sector agencies to sustain and share their substantial body of knowledge and expertise through direct response to survivors and through multi-agency roles, adequate resources are required.
However, like many other third-sector organisations worldwide, their
ability to respond to the ever-increasing demand for their services is
being eroded by a reduction in resources. Amid the recession, many
services report decreased funds at a time of increased demand. SWA,
while not the only specialist service to respond to women and children
affected by domestic abuse, is one of the longest-established and largest
specialist organisations within Scotland. A recent census undertaken
by SWA indicated that their local member groups supported almost
1,000 women with around 350 children in a single day (SWA, 2016a).

Of the thirty-six SWA member organisations, one-third reported that their funding had been reduced in recent years, on average by 15%. Furthermore, those who reported no change to their funding also described this as a reduction in real terms as the funding was not adjusted to reflect inflation (SWA, 2016b). While the Scottish government provides funds through protected VAW funding streams, requiring applicants to demonstrate a gendered analysis of domestic abuse, the future of this level of funding remains uncertain.

Recognising need and meeting demand?

The approach of this book differs from some other texts which consider domestic abuse through dedicating specific chapters to the experiences of different groups of women affected. It is vital that the diverse needs of women are recognised and met. This remains an outstanding challenge in Scotland and elsewhere, partly because of limited peer-reviewed research in this area. In recent years, some pioneering work has been conducted to highlight the distinct experiences and support needs of survivors who are often marginalised within services: for example, the work of LGBT Youth Scotland (2010), which explores the experience of domestic abuse among transgender women; and the work of Mirza (2016), which highlights the interrelated challenges experienced by women from ethnic minorities. Yet there is limited research on issues such as the intersection of disability and domestic abuse.

As discussed in Chapter 7, there is substantial evidence on the negative impact of exposure to domestic abuse for children; thus, domestic abuse is a clear child protection issue. In this context, the role of agencies to consider the needs of children and their mothers is identified. Specifically, for health services through the *National Domestic Abuse Delivery Plan for Children and Young People* (Scottish Government, 2008a) and the Safe and Together Model in children and families' social work services (see Chapter 7). There are challenges to meeting the needs of children and young people exposed to domestic abuse, as discussed in Chapters 6 and 7, but there are also concerns that this focus detracts from the experiences of women who directly experience the abuse and their need for support and protection. Furthermore, the needs of women who are not mothers, or no longer have children in their care, are not recognised within the child protection discourse.

Prevention

Scotland has a proud history of campaigning and preventative work in relation to domestic abuse – and VAW more broadly. Yet, misconceptions about the nature and consequences of domestic abuse persist. In a population-wide survey of attitudes towards violence against women in Scotland, between one-quarter and one-third of respondents considered behaviour such as financial control, stopping a partner from going out or controlling what a partner is wearing as not serious, and that these actions were less likely to have an impact on the partner than physical or verbal abuse (Scottish Government, 2015).

Preventative work in relation to domestic abuse can be broadly divided into two (complementary and interrelated) approaches: initiatives that focus specifically on domestic abuse; and broader efforts to address the gendered inequalities that underpin this abuse. By identifying domestic abuse as a cause and consequence of gender inequality, the argument that addressing inequality would eliminate domestic abuse (and vice versa) follows: 'Until we end violence against women, we cannot have true gender equality, either here in Scotland, or elsewhere around the world' (Nicola Sturgeon, cited in Scottish Government, 2016a, p. 48).

Yet, population level data does not support this theory. One suggestion, discussed by Stark (2007), is that domestic and sexual violence increases as inequality decreases because of a 'backlash' to the attendant increase in freedoms and opportunities for women. For example, countries with greater equality between men and women, such as Germany, ranked second most equal in the world by the United Nations Development Programme (UNDP) (2016), had a reported prevalence of 22% of women who had experienced physical or sexual violence from a partners since the age of fifteen (FRA, 2014). In Denmark, ranked joint fifth for equality by the UNDP, 32% of women reported physical or sexual abuse in the same survey, and in the UK, ranked sixteenth for equality, 29% of women disclosed this abuse (FRA, 2014). While the UK figure is greater than the prevalence disclosed in Germany, it is also marginally higher than countries with greater inequality such as Portugal, ranked forty-first for gender equality but with 19% of women surveyed reporting experience of physical or sexual violence from a partner, or Romania, ranked fiftieth for gender equality but with 24% of women reporting this abuse. However, it is likely that this is the result of challenges in accurately measuring domestic abuse, discussed in Chapter 2, rather than a reflection of the impact of equality on prevalence of abusive behaviour. In particular, it has been suggested that, in countries with greater equality, women are more empowered to recognise and disclose their experiences as abuse (FRA, 2014).

That gender equality does not necessarily guarantee the elimination of domestic abuse indicates that, while efforts to secure equality are laudable in their own right, additional work to address domestic abuse specifically must continue in parallel. Scotland's approach to domestic abuse (and to GBV more generally) has involved a great deal of collaborative working between and across sectors. Efforts to prevent and tackle domestic abuse have been bolstered by feminist research and feminist activism which highlights its nature, extent and impact, and policy efforts to operationalise and implement the findings from research and front-line practice. Since Zero Tolerance's ground-breaking media campaign of the 1990s, a plethora of innovative practice has developed in Scotland in relation to awareness-raising and efforts directed at changing social attitudes, with the ultimate aim of preventing domestic abuse. Examples include: the third sector's active engagement with the media in producing a media toolkit; creating open access images to present alongside media stories of domestic abuse, which challenge the stereotype of a women after physical assault; and the introduction of the 'Write to End Violence Against Women' Awards, which celebrate academic writing and journalism that increases understanding of, or challenges perceptions of domestic abuse. For some time, academics have collaborated with third-sector partners in the Scottish Gender Based Violence Research Network, which brings together academics, activists and practitioners in statutory and specialist services. Currently, the Network has more than 300 members and has organised a range of pioneering events, co-produced a publication on domestic abuse and gender equality (McFeely *et al.*, 2013), and continues to identify – and fill – gaps in the current research evidence base.

Closing comments

This book has attempted to offer both an overview and a critical analysis of Scotland's approach to domestic abuse. Taking a wide-ranging and interdisciplinary lens, it has reflected on a set of key initiatives and reforms, which have animated debate among policymakers, practitioners and academics and, in their enactment, touched many women's lives. There is no doubt that the challenges presented by domestic abuse are daunting, but we have evidence that these are gradually being eroded by the persistent and committed work that is ongoing in Scotland across health, education, social services, criminal and civil justice to bring about cultural and practical change. In view of the challenges discussed within this book, *Equally Safe's* aim of eradicating violence against women in all its forms is, indeed, bold and ambitious. However, as we hope can be seen, there is fertile ground in Scotland for further innovation and change in the future.

REFERENCES

Acker, J. (1990) 'Hierarchies, jobs, bodies: A theory of gendered organisations', *Gender & Society*, Vol. 4, No. 2, pp. 139–58

Alonso, Y. (2004) 'The biopsychosocial model in medical research: The evolution of the health concept over the last two decades', *Patient Education and Counselling*, Vol. 53, No. 2, pp. 239–44

Association of Lecturers and Teachers (2004) *Gender in Education 3–19: A Fresh Approach*, London: Association of Lecturers and Teachers

Avizandum Consultants and AAJ Associates (2009) *Research Report: The Use and Effectiveness of Exclusion Orders under the Matrimonial Homes (Family Protection) (Scotland) Act 1981 in Preventing Homelessness*, Edinburgh: Scottish Women's Aid

Bacchus, L., Bewley, S., Fernandez, C., Hellbernd, H., Lo Fo Wong, S., Otasevic, S., Pas, L., Perttu, S. and Savola, T. (2012) *Health Sector Responses to Domestic Violence in Europe: A Comparison of Promising Intervention Models in Maternity and Primary Care Settings*, London: London School of Hygiene & Tropical Medicine

Bair-Merritt, M. H., Feudtner, C., Localio, A. R., Feinstein, J. A., Rubin, D. and Holmes, W. C. (2008) 'Health care use of children whose female caregivers have intimate partner violence histories', *Archives of Pediatrics & Adolescent Medicine*, Vol. 162, No. 2, pp. 134–9

Barter, C. and Lombard, N. (2017) 'Thinking and doing: Children's and young people's understandings and experiences of intimate partner violence and abuse', in Lombard, N. (ed.) (2018) *Research Companion on Violence Against Women*, Abingdon: Routledge, pp. 287–302

Beauchamp, T. L. and Childress, J. F. (2013) *Principles of Biomedical Ethics*, 7th edn, Oxford: Oxford University Press

Berman, H., Hardesty, J. L., Lewis-O'Connor, A. and Humphreys, J. (2011) 'Childhood exposure to intimate partner violence', in Humphreys, J. and Campbell, J. C., (eds) (2011) *Family Violence and Nursing Practice,* 2nd edn, New York: Springer, pp. 279–318

Bewley, S. and Welch, J. (eds) (2014) *ABC of Domestic and Sexual Violence*, Oxford: Wiley-Blackwell

Bigler, R. S., Hayes, A. R. and Hamilton, V. (2013) 'The role of schools in the early socialization of gender differences', in Tremblay, R. E., Boivin, M. and Peters, R.DeV. (eds) (2013), 'Encyclopedia on early childhood development' (online). Available from URL: www.child-encyclopedia.com/sites/default/files/textes-experts/en/2492/the-role-of-schools-in-the-early-socialization-of-gender-differences.pdf (accessed 5 December 2016)

Blake Stevenson (2011, but not published) *Evaluation of CEL_41 Implementation*. Edinburgh

BMA (1998) *Domestic Abuse: A Health Care Issue?*, London: British Medical Association

BMA (2014) *Domestic Abuse: A Report from the BMA Board of Science*, London: British Medical Association

Brooks, L. (2018) 'Scotland set to pass "gold standard" domestic abuse law', *The Guardian*. Available from URL: www.theguardian.com/society/2018/feb/01/scotland-set-to-pass-gold-standard-domestic-abuse-law (accessed 1 March 2018)

Brooks, O. and Kyle, D. (2015) 'Dual reports of domestic abuse made to the police in Scotland: A summary of findings from a pilot research study' (online), SIPR Research Summary No. 23. Available from URL: www.sccjr.ac.uk/publications/dual-reports-of-domestic-abuse-made-to-the-police-in-scotland-a-summary-of-findings-from-a-pilot-research-study/ (accessed 1 March 2018)

Brooks, O., Burman, M., Lombard, N., McIvor, G., Stevenson-Hastings, L. and Kyle, D. (2014) 'Violence against women: Effective interventions and practices with perpetrators: A literature review' (online), SCCJR Research Report No. 05/2014. Available from URL: www.sccjr.ac.uk/publications/violence-against-women-effective-interventions-and-practices-with-perpetrators/ (accessed 1 March 2018)

Brown, C. (2008) 'Gender-role implications on same-sex intimate partner abuse'. *Journal of Family Violence*, Vol. 23, pp. 457–62

Browning, J. and Dutton, D. (1986) 'Assessment of wife assault with the Conflict Tactics Scale: Using couple data to quantify the differential reporting effect', *Journal of Marriage and the Family*, Vol. 48, No. 2, pp. 375–9

Buckley, H., Holt, S. and Whelan, S. (2007) 'Listen to me! Children's experiences of domestic violence', *Child Abuse Review*, Vol. 16, No. 5, pp. 296–310

Buckley, H., Horwath, J. and Whelan, S. (2006) *Framework for the Assessment of Vulnerable Children and their Families*, Dublin: Children's Research Centre, Trinity College and Sheffield: University of Sheffield

Burman, M. and Brooks-Hay, O. (2018) 'Aligning policy and law? The creation of a domestic abuse offence incorporating coercive control', *Criminology & Criminal Justice*. Available from URL: http://journals.sagepub.com/doi/abs/10.1177/1748895817752223?journalCode=crjb (accessed 1 March 2018)

Burman, M. and Cartmel, F. (2005) *Young People's Attitudes Towards Gendered Violence*, Edinburgh: NHS Health Scotland

Burman, M. and Johnstone, J. (2015) 'High hopes? The gender equality duty and its impact on responses to gender-based violence', *Policy & Politics*, Vol. 43, No. 1, pp. 45–60

Burman, M. and MacQueen, S. (2015) *A Pre-Evaluation Review of the Caledonian System*, SCCJR Research Report, Glasgow: Scottish Centre for Crime and Justice Research

Burman, M., Jamieson, L., Nicholson, J. and Brooks, O. (2007) *Impact of Aspects of the Law of Evidence in Sexual Offence Trials: An Evaluation Study*, Edinburgh: Scottish Executive

Burton, M. (2008) *Legal Responses to Domestic Abuse*, Abingdon: Routledge Cavendish

Burton, M. (2016) 'A fresh approach to policing domestic violence', in Hilder, S.

and Bettinson, V. (eds) (2016) *Domestic Violence*, London: Palgrave Macmillan, pp. 37–57

Burton, S., Kitzinger, J., Kelly, L. and Regan, L. (1998) *Young People's Attitudes Towards Violence, Sex and Relationships: A Survey and Focus Group Study*, London and Glasgow: Child and Woman Abuse Study Unit, University of London and the Media Research Unit, Sociology Department, University of Glasgow: Zero Tolerance Charitable Trust

Buzawa, E. S. and Buzawa, C. G. (2003) *Domestic Violence: The Criminal Justice Response*, London: Sage

Cairney, P., Russell., S and St Denny, E. (2016) 'The "Scottish approach" to policy and policymaking: What issues are territorial and what are universal?', *Policy & Politics*, Vol. 44, No. 3, pp. 333–50

Campbell, J. C. (2004) 'Helping women understand their risk in situations of intimate partner violence', *Journal of Interpersonal Violence*, Vol. 19, No. 12, pp. 1464–77

Campbell, J. C., Webster, D. W. and Glass. N. (2009) 'The danger assessment: Validation of a lethality risk assessment instrument for intimate partner femicide', *Journal of Interpersonal Violence*, Vol. 24, No. 4, pp. 653–74

Cavanagh, K., Connelly, C. and Scoular, J. (2003) *An Evaluation of the Protection from Abuse (Scotland) Act 2001*, Edinburgh: Scottish Executive Social Research

Chantler, K., Baker, V., MacKenzie, M., McCarry, M. and Mirza, N. (2017) *Understanding Forced Marriage in Scotland: Equality, Poverty and Social Security*, Edinburgh: Scottish Government

Chantler, K., Gangoli, G. and Hester, M. (2009) 'Forced marriage in the UK: Religious, cultural, economic or state violence?', *Critical Social Policy*, Vol. 29, No. 4, pp. 587–612

Charles, N. and Mackay, F. (2013) 'Feminist politics and framing contests: Domestic violence policy in Scotland and Wales', *Critical Social Policy*, Vol. 33, No. 4, pp. 593–615

Children (Scotland) Act (1995) 'Chapter 36' (online). Available from URL: www. legislation.gov.uk/ukpga/1995/36/pdfs/ukpga_19950036_en.pdf (accessed 26 November 2017)

Children and Young People (Scotland) Act (2014) '2014 asp.8' (online). Available from URL: www.legislation.gov.uk/asp/2014/8/pdfs/asp_20140008_en.pdf (accessed 23 November 2017)

Children's Hearings (Scotland) Act (2011) '2011 asp.1' (online). Available from URL: www.legislation.gov.uk/asp/2011/1/pdfs/asp_20110001_en.pdf (accessed 26 November 2017)

City of Edinburgh Council (2017) 'Safe and Together Edinburgh' (online), The City of Edinburgh Council, Corporate Policy and Strategy Committee. Available from URL www.edinburgh.gov.uk/info/20110/domestic_abuse/1462/safe_ and_together_edinburgh (accessed 1 March 2018)

Cleaver, H., Nicholson, D., Tarr, S. and Cleaver, D. (2007) *Child Protection, Domestic Violence and Parental Substance Misuse: Family Experiences and Effective Practice*, London: Jessica Kingsley

Connell, R. W. (1987) *Gender and Power: Society, the Person and Sexual Politics*, Cambridge: Polity Press in association with Blackwell Publishers

Connell, R. W. and Messerschmidt, J. W. (2005) 'Hegemonic masculinity: Rethinking the concept', *Gender & Society,* Vol. 19, No. 6, pp. 829–59

Connelly, C. (2011) 'Specialist responses to domestic abuse', in Hughes, H. (ed.) (2011) *Domestic Abuse and Scots Law,* Edinburgh: W. Green

Connelly, C. and Cavanagh, K. (2007) 'Domestic abuse, civil protection orders and the "new criminologies": Is there any value in engaging with the law?', *Feminist Legal Studies,* Vol. 15, pp. 259–87

Cook, D., Burton, M., Robinson, A. and Vallely, C. (2004) *Evaluation of Specialist Domestic Violence Courts/Fast Track Systems,* London: Crown Prosecution Service and Department of Constitutional Affairs

COPFS (2017) *Domestic Abuse Charges Reported to COPFS 2016–2017.* Edinburgh: Crown Office and Prosecutor Service. Available from URL: www.copfs.gov.uk/images/Documents/Publications/Statistics%20-%20 Domestic%20Abuse/DOMESTIC%20ABUSE%20CHARGES%20 REPORTED%20TO%20COPFS%202016-17%20Word.pdf (accessed 21 March 2018)

Cordis Bright Consulting (2011) *Research into Multi-Agency Assessment Conferences (MARACs),* London: Home Office

Council of Europe (2002) *Recommendation of the Committee of Ministers to Member States on the Protection of Women Against Violence,* Adopted on 30 April 2002; and Explanatory Memorandum, Strasbourg, France: Council of Europe

Coy, M., Kelly, L. and Foord, J. (2007) *Map of Gaps: The Postcode Lottery of Violence Against Women Support Services in the UK,* London: End Violence Against Women Coalition

Cuthbert, J. and Irving, L. (2001) 'Women's aid in Scotland: Purity versus pragmatism?', in Breitenbach, E. and Mackay, F. (eds) (2001) *Women and Contemporary Scottish Politics,* Edinburgh: Polygon, pp. 55–68

Davies, P. A. and Biddle, P. (2017). 'Implementing a perpetrator-focused partnership approach to tackling domestic abuse: The opportunities and challenges of criminal justice localism', *Criminology & Criminal Justice.* Available from URL: http://journals.sagepub.com/doi/ abs/10.1177/1748895817734590 (accessed 1 March 2018)

DeLeon-Granados, W., Wells, W. and Binsbacher, R. (2006) 'Arresting developments: Trends in female arrests for domestic violence and proposed explanations', *Violence Against Women,* Vol. 12, No. 4, pp. 355–71

Devaney, J. (2008) 'Chronic child abuse and domestic violence: Children and families with long-term and complex needs', *Child & Family Social Work,* Vol. 13, No. 4, pp. 443–53

Devaney, J. (2015) 'Research review: The impact of domestic violence on children', *Irish Probation Journal,* Vol. 12, pp. 79–94

DMSS Research (2015) 'An independent evaluation of Rape Crisis Scotland's violence prevention project' (online). Available from URL: www. rapecrisisscotland.org.uk/resources/final-evaluation-report-26-04.pdf (accessed 21 March 2018)

Dobash, R. E. and Dobash, R. P. (1979) *Violence Against Wives: A Case Against the Patriarchy,* New York, NY: Free Press

Dobash, R. E. and Dobash, R. P. (1992) *Women, Violence and Social*

Change, London: Routledge

Dobash, R. E. and Dobash, R. P. (2015) *When Men Murder Women,* Oxford: Oxford University Press

Dobash, R. E., Dobash, R., Cavanagh, K. and Lewis, R. (2000) *Changing Violent Men,* London: Sage

Dobash, R. P. and Dobash, R. E. (2004) 'Women's violence to men in intimate relationships: Working on a puzzle', *British Journal of Criminology,* Vol. 44, No. 3, pp. 324–49

Dobash, R. P., Dobash, R. E., Cavanagh, K. and Lewis, R. (1996) *Research Evaluation of Programmes for Violent Men,* Edinburgh: Scottish Office Central Research Unit.

DoH (2010) *Responding to Violence Against Women and Children: The Role of the NHS,* London: Department of Health

Donovan, C. and Hester, M. (2010) ' "I hate the word 'victim' ": An exploration of recognition of domestic violence in same sex relationships', *Social Policy and Society,* Vol. 9, No. 2, pp. 279–89

Dublin Women's Aid (1999) *Teenage Tolerance: The Hidden Lives of Young Irish People: A Study of Young People's Experiences and Responses to Violence and Abuse,* Dublin: Women's Aid

Duggan, M. (2012) 'Using victims' voices to prevent violence against women: A critique', *British Journal of Community Justice,* Vol. 10, No. 2, pp. 25–37

Eckhardt, C., Murphy, C., Whitaker, D., Sprunger, J., Dykstra, R. and Woodard, J. (2013) 'The effectiveness of intervention programmes for perpetrators and victims of intimate partner violence', *Partner Abuse,* Vol. 4, No. 2, pp. 196–231

Education (Scotland) Act (2014) '2016 asp.8' (online). Available from URL: www.legislation.gov.uk/asp/2016/8/pdfs/asp_20160008_en.pdf (accessed 24 November 2017)

Edwards, S. (1989) *Policing Domestic Violence: Women, the Law and the State,* London: Sage

Elliot, P. (1996) 'Shattering illusions: Same-sex domestic violence', *Journal of Gay and Lesbian Social Service,* Vol. 4, No. 1, pp. 1–8

Equality Act (2010) 'Chapter 15' (online). Available from URL: www.legislation. gov.uk/ukpga/2010/15/pdfs/ukpga_20100015_en.pdf (accessed 8 December 2016)

Evans, S. E., Davies, C. and DiLillo, D. (2008) 'Exposure to domestic violence: A meta-analysis of child and adolescent outcomes', *Aggression and Violent Behavior,* Vol. 13, No. 2, pp. 131–40

EVAW (2011) *A Different World is Possible: A call for long-term and targeted action to prevent violence against women and girls,* London: End Violence Against Women Coalition. Available from URL: www.endviolenceagainstwomen.org.uk/wp-content/uploads/a_different_world_is_possible_report_email_version. pdf (accessed 16 March 2018)

Farrell, G. and Pease, K. (2010) 'The sting in the tail of the British Crime Survey', in Hough, M. and Maxfield, M. (eds) (2010) *Crime in the Twenty-First Century,* Boulder, CO: Lynne Rienner Publishers

Feder, G., Ramsay, J., Dunne, D., Rose, M., Arsene, C., Norman, R., Kuntze, S., Spencer, A., Bacchus, L., Hague, G., Warburton, A. and Taket, A. (2009) 'How far does screening women for domestic (partner) violence in different health-care settings meet criteria for a screening programme? Systematic reviews of nine UK National Screening Committee criteria', *Health Technol Assess,* Vol. 13, No. 16; doi: 10.3310/hta13160

Fielding, N. (1994) 'Cop canteen culture', in Newburn, T. A. and Stanko, E. A. (eds) (1994) *Just Boys Doing Business? Men, Masculinities and Crime,* London: Routledge, pp. 46–63

Fitzgibbon, K. and Walklate, S. (2016) 'The efficacy of Clare's Law in domestic violence reform in England and Wales', *Criminology & Criminal Justice,* Vol. 17, No. 3, pp. 1–17

Ford, D. A. (1983) 'Wife battery and criminal justice: A study of victim decision-making', *Family Relations,* Vol. 21, No. 4, pp. 463–75

FRA (European Union Agency for Fundamental Rights) (2014) *Violence Against Women: An EU Wide Survey – Main Results Report,* Luxembourg: Publication Office of the European Union

Freire, P. (1996) *Pedagogy of the Oppressed,* London: Penguin

GMC (2013) *Good Medical Practice,* Manchester: General Medical Council

Gorin, S. (2004) *Understanding What Children Say: Children's Experiences of Domestic Violence, Parental Substance Misuse and Parental Health Problems,* London: National Children's Bureau

Grace, J. (2015) 'Clare's Law, or the national domestic violence disclosure scheme: The contested legalities of criminality information sharing', *Journal of Criminal Law,* Vol. 79, No. 1, pp. 36–45

Griffiths, S. (2000) 'Women, anger and domestic violence: The implications for legal defences to murder', in Hanmer, J. and Itzin, C. (eds) (2000) *Home Truths about Domestic Violence: Feminist Influences on Policy and Practice,* London: Routledge

Groves, N. and Thomas, T. (2014) *Domestic Violence and Criminal Justice,* Abingdon: Routledge

Hanmer, J. and Saunders, S. (1984) *Well-Founded Fear: A Community Study of Violence to Women,* London: Hutchinson

HCPC (2016) *Standards of Conduct, Performance and Ethics,* London: Health and Care Professions Council

Healthy Respect (2016) 'Young people's views on their school-based Relationships, Sexual Health and Parenthood Education (RSHPE): Summary report for Healthy Respect' (online). Available from URL: www.healthyrespect. co.uk/Professionals/HealthyRespectNetworks/Documents/HR%20NHS%20 (TASC%20Report).pdf (accessed 25 November 2017)

Hearn, J. (1998) *The Violences of Men: How Men Talk About and How Agencies Respond to Men's Violence to Women,* London: Sage

Hearn, J. and McKie, L. (2010) 'Gendered and social hierarchies in problem representation and policy processes: "Domestic Violence" in Finland and Scotland', *Violence Against Women,* Vol. 16, No. 2, pp. 136–58

Henderson, L. (2003) *Prevalence of Domestic Violence Among Lesbians and Gay Men,* London: Sigma Research

Hester, M. (2004) 'Future trends and developments: Violence against women in Europe and East Asia', *Violence Against Women,* Vol. 10, No. 12, pp. 1431–1448

Hester, M. (2009) *Who Does What to Whom? Gender and Domestic Violence Perpetrators,* Bristol: University of Bristol in Association with the Northern Rock Foundation

Hester, M. (2011) 'Portrayal of women as intimate partner domestic violence perpetrators', *Violence Against Women,* Vol. 18, No. 9, pp. 1067–82

Hester, M. (2013) 'Who does what to whom? Gender and domestic violence perpetrators in English police records', *European Journal of Criminology,* Vol. 10, No. 5, pp. 623–37

Hester, M., Pearce, J. and Westmarland, N. (2008) *Early Evaluation of the Integrated Domestic Violence Court, Croydon,* Ministry of Justice Research Series 18/08, London: Ministry of Justice

HMIC (2014) 'Everyone's business: Improving the police response to domestic abuse' (online). Available from URL: www.hmic.gov.uk/wp-content/uploads/2014/04/improving-the-police-response-to-domestic-abuse.pdf (accessed 1 March 2018)

Holden, G. A. (2003) 'Children exposed to domestic violence and child abuse: Terminology and taxonomy', *Clinical Child and Family Psychology Review,* Vol. 6, No. 3, pp. 151–60

Holland, J., Ramazanoglu, C., Sharpe, S. and Thomson, R. (2004) *The Male in the Head: Young People, Heterosexuality and Power,* 2nd edn, London: Tufnel Press

Holt, S. (2015), 'Post-separation fathering and domestic abuse: Challenges and contradictions: Post-separation fathering and domestic violence', *Child Abuse Review,* Vol. 24, No. 3, pp. 210–22

Holt, S., Buckley, H. and Whelan, S. (2008) 'The impact of exposure to domestic violence on children and young people: A review of the literature', *Child Abuse & Neglect,* Vol. 32, No. 8, pp. 797–810

Holt, V. A., Kernic, M. A., Wolf, M. E. and Rivera, F. P. (2003) 'Do protection orders affect the likelihood of future partner violence', *American Journal of Preventative Medicine,* Vol. 21, No. 1, pp. 16–21

Hornor, G. (2005) 'Domestic violence and children', *Journal of Pediatric Health Care,* Vol. 19, No. 4, pp. 206–12

Howarth, E. and Robinson, A. (2016) 'Responding effectively to women experiencing severe abuse: Identifying key components of a British advocacy intervention', *Violence Against Women,* Vol. 22, No. 1, pp. 41–63

Hoyle, C. (1998) *Negotiating Domestic Violence: Police, Criminal Justice, and Victims,* Oxford: Clarendon

Hoyle, C. and Sanders, A. (2000) 'Police response to domestic violence: From victim choice to victim empowerment?', *British Journal of Criminology,* Vol. 40, No. 1, pp. 14–36

Humphreys, C. and Bradbury-Jones, C. (2015) 'Domestic abuse and safeguarding children: Focus, response and intervention', *Child Abuse Review,* Vol. 24, No. 4, pp. 231–34

Humphreys, C. and Thiara, R. (2003) 'Mental health and domestic violence: "I call it symptoms of abuse" ', *The British Journal of Social Work,* Vol. 33, No. 2, pp. 209–26

Humphreys, C., Houghton, C. and Ellis, J. (2008) *Literature Review: Better Outcomes for Children and Young People Experiencing Domestic Abuse – Directions for Good Practice,* Edinburgh: Scottish Government

Jaffe, P., Wolfe, D. and Wilson, S. (1990) *Children of Battered Women,* London: Sage

Johnson, H. and Sacco, V. F. (1995) 'Researching violence against women: Statistics Canada's national survey', *Canadian Journal of Criminology,* Vol. 37, pp. 281–304

Johnson, M. (2008) *A Typology of Domestic Violence: Intimate Terrorism, Violent Resistances, and Situational Couple Violence,* Boston, MA: University Press of New England

Johnson, M. P. (1995) 'Patriarchal terrorism and common couple violence: Two forms of violence against women', *Journal of Marriage and the Family,* Vol. 57, No. 2, pp. 283–94

Johnson, M. P. and Ferraro, K. J. (2000) 'Research on domestic violence in the 1990s: Making distinctions', *Journal of Marriage and Family,* Vol. 62, No. 4, pp. 948–63

Katz, E. (2015) 'Recovery-promoters: Ways in which children and mothers support one another's recoveries from domestic violence', *British Journal of Social Work,* Vol. 45, No. 1, pp. i153-i169; doi: 10.1093/bjsw/bcv091

Katz, J. (1995) 'Reconstructing masculinity in the locker room: The mentors in violence prevention project', *Harvard Educational Review,* Vol. 65, No. 2, pp. 163–75

Keeling, J. and Fisher, C. (2015) 'Health professionals' responses to women's disclosure of domestic violence', *Journal of Interpersonal Violence,* Vol. 30, No. 13, pp. 2363–78

Kelly, L. (1988) *Surviving Sexual Violence,* Cambridge: Polity Press

Kelly, L. (1999) 'Violence against women: A policy of neglect or a neglect of policy?', in Walby, S. (ed.) (1999), *New Agendas for Women,* London: Macmillan Press, pp. 119–47

Kelly, L., Hagemann-White, C., Meysen, T. and Römkens, R. (2011) *Realising Rights: Case Studies on State Responses to Violence Against Women and Children in Europe,* London: Child and Woman Abuse Unit and London Metropolitan University

Kelly, L., Regan, L. and Burton, S. (1991) *An Exploratory Study of the Prevalence of Sexual Abuse in a Sample of 16–21 Year Olds,* London: Child Abuse Studies Unit, University of North London

Kelly, L., and Westmarland, N. (2015a) *Domestic Violence Perpetrator Programmes: Steps Towards Change: Project Mirabal Final Report,* London and Durham: London Metropolitan University and Durham University

Kelly, L. and Westmarland, N. (2015b) 'New approaches to assessing effectiveness and outcomes of domestic violence perpetrator programmes', in Johnson, H., Fisher, B. S. and Jaquier, V. (eds) (2015) *Critical Issues on Violence Against Women,* Abingdon: Routledge, pp. 183–94

Kelly, L. and Westmarland, N. (2016) 'Naming and defining "Domestic violence": Lessons from research with violent men', *Feminist review,* Vol. 112, No. 1, pp. 113–27

Kethineni, S. and Beichner, D. (2009) 'A comparison of civil and criminal orders of protection as remedies for domestic violence victims in a Midwestern county', *Journal of Family Violence,* Vol. 24, No. 5, pp. 311–21

Kitzmann, K. M., Gaylord, N. K., Holt, A. R. and Kenny, E. D. (2003) 'Child witnesses to domestic violence: A meta-analytic review', *Journal of Consulting Clinical Psychology*, Vol. 71, No. 2, pp. 339–52

Ko, C. N. (2002) 'Civil restraining orders for domestic violence: The unresolved question of "efficacy" ', *Southern California Interdisciplinary Law Journal*, Vol. 11, No. 2, pp. 361–90

Krug, E. G., Dahlberg, L. L., Mercy, J. A., Zwi, A. B. and Rafael, L. (2002) *The World Report on Violence and Health*, Geneva: World Health Organization

Laing, L., Humphreys, C., and Cavanagh, K. (2013) *Social Work and Domestic Violence: Developing Critical and Reflective Practice*, London: Sage

Levendosky, A. A., Huth-Bocks, A. and Semel, M. A. (2002) 'Adolescent peer relationships and mental health functioning in families with domestic violence', :*Journal of Clinical Child & Adolescent Psychology*, Vol. 31, No. 2, pp. 206–18

LGBT Youth Scotland (2010) 'Out of sight, out of mind: Transgender people's experiences of domestic abuse' (online). Available from URL: www.lgbtyouth. org.uk/files/documents/DomesticAbuseResources/transgender_DA.pdf (accessed 1 March 2018)

Logan, T. K., Stevenson, E., Evans, L. and Leukefeld, C. (2004) 'Rural and urban women's perceptions of barriers to health, mental health, and criminal justice services: Implications for victim services', *Violence and victims*, Vol. 19, No. 1; pp. 37–62

Logan, T. and Walker, R (2010) 'Civil protection order effectiveness: Justice or just a piece of paper?', *Violence and Victims*, Vol. 25, No. 3, pp. 332–48

Lombard, N. (2013) 'Young people's temporal and spatial accounts of gendered violence', *Sociology*, Vol. 47, No. 6, pp. 1136–51

Lombard, N. (2014) ' "Because they're a couple she should do what he says": Justifications of violence: Heterosexuality, gender and adulthood', *Journal of Gender Studies*, Vol. 25, No. 3, pp. 241–53. Available from URL: www. tandfonline.com/doi/abs/10.1080/09589236.2014.943699 (accessed 1 March 2018)

Lombard, N. (2015) *Young People's Understandings of Men's Violence Against Women*, Farnham: Ashgate

Lombard, N. and Whiting, N. (2015) 'Domestic abuse: Feminism, the government and the unique case of Scotland', in Goel, R. and Goodmark, L. (eds) (2015) *Comparative Perspectives on Domestic Violence: Lessons from Efforts Worldwide*, Oxford: Oxford University Press, pp. 155–68

Lynch, K. and Feeley, M. (2009) 'Gender and education (and employment): Gendered imperatives and their implications for women and men: Lessons from research for policy makers' (online), an independent report submitted to the European Commission by the NESSE network of experts. Available from URL: www.nesse.fr/nesse/activities/reports/activities/reports/gender-report-pdf (accessed 26 November 2017)

McCarry, M. (2003) 'The connection between masculinity and domestic violence: What young people think' (unpublished PhD), Bristol: University of Bristol

McCarry, M., Donovan, C., Hester, M. and Holmes, J. (2006) *Comparing Domestic Abuse in Same Sex and Heterosexual Relationships*, Bristol: University of Bristol

McCloskey, L. A., Lichter, E., Williams, C., Gerber, N., Wittenberg, E. and Ganz, M. (2006) 'Assessing intimate partner violence in health care settings leads to women's receipt of interventions and improved health', *Public Health Reports*, Vol. 121, No. 4, pp. 435–44

McCue, M. L. (2008) *Domestic Violence: A Reference Handbook*, Santa Barbara, CA: ABC-CLIO Inc

McFeely, C. (2016) 'The health visitor response to domestic abuse' (unpublished PhD), Glasgow: University of Glasgow

McFeely, C., Whiting, N., Lombard, N., Brooks, O. Burman, M. and McGowan, M. (2013) *Domestic Abuse and Gender Inequality: An Overview of the Current Debate*, Briefing 69, Edinburgh: Centre for Families and Relationships, University of Edinburgh

McGee, C. (1997) 'Children's experiences of domestic violence', *Child and Family Social Work*, Vol. 2, pp. 13–23

McGee, C. (2000) *Childhood Experiences of Domestic Violence*, London: Jessica Kingsley

McIvor G (2009) 'Therapeutic jurisprudence and procedural justice in Scottish drug courts', *Criminology & Criminal Justice*, Vol. 9, No. 1, pp. 29–49

Mackay, F. (1996) 'The Zero Tolerance campaign: Setting the agenda', *Parliamentary Affairs*, Vol. 49, No. 1, pp. 206–20

Mackay, F. (2010) 'Gendering constitutional change and policy outcomes: Substantive representation and domestic violence policy in Scotland', *Policy & Politics*, Vol. 38, No. 3, pp. 369–88

McMillan, L. (2015) 'The role of the specially trained officer in rape and sexual offence cases', *Policing and Society*, Vol. 25, No. 6, pp. 622–40

MacQueen, S. (2013) *Domestic Violence and Victim/Police Interaction*, SIPR Annual Report. Available from URL: http://library.college.police.uk/docs/MacQueen-Domestic-Violence-Police-Victim-Interaction-summary-2015.pdf (accessed 1 March 2018)

MacQueen, S. (2016) 'Domestic abuse, crime surveys and the fallacy of risk: Exploring partner and domestic abuse using the Scottish Crime and Justice Survey', *Criminology & Criminal Justice*, Vol. 16, No. 4, pp. 470–496

MacQueen, S. and Norris, P. A. (2014) 'Police awareness and involvement in cases of domestic and partner abuse', *Policing in Society: An international Journal of Research and Policy*, Vol. 26, No. 1, pp. 55–76. Available from URL: www.tandfonline.com/doi/abs/10.1080/10439463.2014.922084 (accessed 1 March 2018)

Malterud, K. (2001) 'The art and science of clinical knowledge: Evidence beyond measures and numbers', *The Lancet*, Vol. 358, No. 9279, pp. 397–400

Mandel, D. (2014) 'Safe and Together Model: Overview and evaluation data briefing' (online). Available from URL: www.endingviolence.com/wp-content/uploads/2013/01/2015Overview-and-Evidence-Briefing-October-2014.pdf (accessed 6 September 2017)

Manjoo, R. and Nadj, D. (2015) ' "Bridging the divide": An interview with Professor Rashida Manjoo, UN Special Rapporteur on violence against women', *Feminist Legal Studies*, Vol. 23, No. 3, pp. 329–47

Matczak, A. Hatzidimitriadou, E. and Lindsay, J. (2011) *Review of Domestic*

Violence policies in England and Wales. London: Kingston University and St George's, University of London

Meltzer, H., Doos, L., Vostanis, P., Ford, T. and Goodman, R. (2009) 'The mental health of children who witness domestic violence', *Child & Family Social Work*, Vol. 14, No. 4, pp. 491–501

Millward, L. M., Kelly, M. P. and Nutbeam, D. (2003) *Public Health Intervention Research: The Evidence,* London: Health Development Agency

Mirza, N. (2016) *South Asian Women's Experience of Family Abuse: The Role of the Husband's Mother,* Briefing 80, Edinburgh: Centre for Research on Families and Relationships, University of Edinburgh

Moe, A. (2000) 'Battered women in the restraining order process', *Violence Against Women*, Vol. 6, No. 6, pp. 606–32

Morran, D. (2013) 'Desisting from domestic abuse: Influences, patterns and processes in the lives of formerly abusive men', *The Howard Journal of Criminal Justice*, Vol. 52, No. 3, pp. 306–20

Morrison, F. (2014) 'Children, contact and domestic abuse' (unpublished PhD), Edinburgh: University of Edinburgh

Morrison, F., Tisdall, E. K. M., Jones, F. and Reid, A. (2013) *Child Contact Proceedings for Children Affected by Domestic Abuse,* Edinburgh: Scotland's Commissioner for Children and Young People

Mullender, A. and Burton, L. (2001) 'Good practice with perpetrators of domestic violence', *Probation Journal*, Vol. 48, No. 4, pp. 260–26

Mullender, A., Hague, G., Imam, U. F., Kelly, L., Malos, E. and Regan, L. (2002) *Children's Perspectives on Domestic Violence,* London: Sage

Murray, K. (2016) *Scottish Crime and Justice Survey 2014/15: Partner Abuse,* Edinburgh: Scottish Government

Myhill, A. (2017) 'Measuring domestic violence: Context is everything', *Journal of Gender-Based Violence*, Vol. 1, No. 1, pp. 33–44

Myhill, A. and Johnson, K. (2016) 'Police use of discretion in response to domestic violence', *Criminology & Criminal Justice*, Vol. 16, No. 1, pp. 3–20

National GBV and Health Programme (2011 but not published) *Evaluation of Routine Enquiry of Domestic Abuse Training Programme: Focus Group Findings,* Evaluation Report for Scottish Government, Edinburgh

National GBV and Health Programme (2012 but not published) *Evaluating Service User Views of Routine Enquiry of Abuse in Health Settings,* Evaluation Report for Scottish Government, Edinburgh

NHS Scotland and Scottish Government (2011) *Asking About Abuse: Routine enquiry of domestic abuse for sexual and reproductive health, A&E, maternity and community nursing,* Training Pack, Edinburgh

NICE (2014) *Domestic Violence and Abuse: Multi-Agency Working,* PH50, London: National Institute for Health and Care Excellence

Nichols, A. (2013) 'Meaning-making and domestic violence victim advocacy: An examination of feminist identities, ideologies, and practices', *Feminist Criminology*, Vol. 8, No. 3, pp. 177–201

NMC (2015a) *The Code: Professional Standards of Conduct and Behaviours for Nurses and Midwives,* London: Nursing and Midwifery Council

NMC (2015b) *Raising Concerns: Guidance for Nurses and Midwives,* London:

Nursing and Midwifery Council

O'Doherty, L. J., Taft, A., Hegarty, K., Ramsay, J., Davidson, L. L. and Feder, G. (2014) 'Screening women for intimate partner violence in healthcare settings: Abridged Cochrane systematic review and meta-analysis', *British Medical Journal*, 348:g2913; doi: 10.1136/bmj.g2913

Ormston, R., Mullholland, C. and Setterfield, L. (2016) *Caledonian System Evaluation: Analysis of a Programme for Tackling Domestic Abuse in Scotland*, Crime and Justice Social Research, Edinburgh: Scottish Government

Øverlien, C. and Hydén, M. (2009) 'Children's actions when experiencing domestic violence', *Childhood*, Vol. 16, No. 4, pp. 479–96

Pain, R. (2012) *Everyday Terrorism: How Fear Works in Domestic Abuse*, Durham: Centre for Social Justice and Community Action, Durham University and Scottish Women's Aid

Peckover, S. (2014) 'Domestic abuse, safeguarding children and public health: Towards an analysis of discursive forms and surveillant techniques in contemporary UK policy and practice', *British Journal of Social Work*, Vol. 44, No. 7, pp. 1770–87

Peckover, S. and Trotter, F. (2015) 'Keeping the focus on children: The challenges of safeguarding children affected by domestic abuse', *Health & Social Care in the Community*, Vol. 23, No. 4, pp. 399–407

Pence, E. and Paymar, M. (1993) Education Groups for Men Who Batter: The Duluth Model, New York, NY: Springer

Pitman, T. (2017) 'Living with coercive control: Trapped within a complex web of double standards, double binds and boundary violations', *British Journal of Social Work*, Vol. 47, No. 1, pp. 143–61

Police Scotland (2016) 'First anniversary of Disclosure Scheme for domestic abuse. 1st October 2016' (online). Available at URL: www.scotland.police.uk/ whats-happening/news/2016/october/first-anniversary-of-disclosure-scheme-for-domestic-abuse-scotland (accessed 16 March 2018)

Police Scotland (2017) 'Second anniversary of Disclosure Scheme for domestic abuse. 1st October 2017' (online). Available at URL: www.scotland.police. uk/whats-happening/news/2017/september/second-anniversary-disclosure-scheme-domestic-abuse-scotland (accessed 16 March 2018)

Police Scotland and COPFS (2013) 'Joint protocol between Police Scotland and Crown Office and Procurator Fiscal Service: In partnership challenging domestic abuse' (online), 3rd edn. Available from URL: www.copfs.gov. uk/images/Documents/Prosecution_Policy_Guidance/Protocols_and_ Memorandum_of_Understanding/Joint%20Domestic%20Abuse%20 Protocol%20-%20Oct%2013.pdf (accessed 1 March 2018)

Police Scotland and COPFS (2017) 'Joint protocol between Police Scotland and the Crown Office and Procurator Fiscal Service: In partnership challenging domestic abuse' (online), 4th edn. Available at URL: www.scotland.police.uk/ assets/pdf/keep_safe/175573?view=Standard (accessed 25 November 2017)

Priestley, M. (2013) 'The 3–18 curriculum in Scottish education', in Bryce, T. G. K., Humes, W. M., Gillies, D. and Kennedy, A. (eds) (2013) *Scottish Education: Referendum*, 4th edn, Edinburgh: Edinburgh University Press, pp. 28–38

Radford, L., Corral, S., Bradley, C., Fisher, H., Bassett, C., Howat, N. and Collishaw,

S. (2011), *Child Abuse and Neglect in the UK Today,* London: National Society for the Prevention of Cruelty to Children

Radford, L. and Hester, M. (2006) *Mothering Through Domestic Violence,* London: Jessica Kingsley

RCM (2006) *Domestic Abuse in Pregnancy: A Position Paper,* London: Royal College of Midwives

RCOG (1997) *Recommendations Arising from the Study Group on Violence Against Women,* London: Royal College Obstetricians and Gynaecologists

Reid, S., McConville, S., Wild, A., Burman, M. and Curtice, J. (2015) *Scottish Social Attitudes Survey 2014: Attitudes to Violence Against Women,* Scottish Government Social Research, Edinburgh: Scottish Government

Reid Howie Associates (2002) *Evaluation of the Zero Tolerance 'Respect' Pilot,* Edinburgh: Scottish Executive

Reid Howie Associates (2007) *Evaluation of the Pilot Domestic Abuse Court,* Edinburgh: Scottish Executive

Robertson, A. (2014) 'Domestic abuse court to be extended', *Holyrood Magazine.* Available from URL: www.holyrood.com/articles/news/domestic-abuse-court-be-extended (accessed 1 March 2018)

Robinson, A. (2007) 'Improving the civil-criminal interface for victims of domestic violence', *The Howard Journal of Criminal Justice,* Vol. 46, No. 4, pp. 356–71

Robinson, A. and Hudson, K. (2011) 'Different yet complementary: Two approaches to supporting victims of sexual violence in the UK', *Criminology & Criminal Justice,* Vol. 11, No. 5, pp. 515–33

Robinson A. and Payton J. (2016) 'Independent advocacy and multi-agency responses to domestic violence', in Hilder, S. and Bettinson, V. (eds) (2016) *Domestic Violence,* London: Palgrave Macmillan

Robinson, A. L. (2004) *Domestic Violence MARACs (Multi-Agency Risk Assessment Conferences) For Very High Right Victims in Cardiff, Wales: A Process and Outcome Evaluation,* Cardiff: Cardiff University

Robinson, A. L., Myhill, A. and Wire, J. (2017) 'Practitioner (mis)understandings of coercive control in England and Wales', *Criminology & Criminal Justice,* Vol. 18, No. 1. Available from URL: http://journals.sagepub.com/doi/abs/10.1177/1748895817728381 (accessed 1 March 2018)

Robinson, A. L. and Tregidga, J. (2007) 'The perceptions of high-risk victims of domestic violence to a coordinated community response in Cardiff, Wales', *Violence Against Women,* Vol. 13, No. 11, pp. 1130–48

SafeLives (2014) 'Dash risk checklist for the identification of high risk cases of domestic abuse, stalking and "honour"-based violence' (online). Available at URL: www.safelives.org.uk/sites/default/files/resources/Dash%20for%20IDVAs%20FINAL.pdf (accessed 25 November 2017).

SafeLives (2017) 'Whole lives: Improving the response to domestic abuse in Scotland' (online). Available from URL: www.safelives.org.uk/sites/default/files/resources/Whole%20Lives_Improving%20the%20response%20to%20domestic%20abuse%20in%20Scotland.pdf (accessed 25 November 2017)

Scott, M. (2004) *Older Women and Domestic Violence in Scotland,* Briefing 39, Edinburgh: Centre for Research on Families and Relationships, University of Edinburgh

Scottish Executive (2000) *Scottish Partnership on Domestic Abuse: National Strategy to Address Domestic Abuse in Scotland*, Edinburgh: Scottish Executive

Scottish Executive (2001) *Preventing Violence Against Women: Action Across the Scottish Executive*, Edinburgh: Scottish Executive

Scottish Executive (2003) *A National Strategy for the Prevention of Domestic Abuse*, Edinburgh: Scottish Executive.

Scottish Government (2007) *Better Health, Better Care Action Plan*, Edinburgh: Scottish Government

Scottish Government (2008a) *National Domestic Abuse Delivery Plan for Children and Young People*, Edinburgh: Scottish Government

Scottish Government (2008b) *Chief Executive's Letter 41: Gender-Based Violence Action Plans*, CEL 41, Edinburgh: Scottish Government

Scottish Government (2008c) *Building the Curriculum 3: A Framework for Learning and Teaching*, Edinburgh: Scottish Government

Scottish Government (2009) *Safer Lives, Changed Lives: A Shared Approach to Tackling Violence Against Women*, Edinburgh: Scottish Government

Scottish Government (2010) *The Healthcare Quality Strategy for NHS Scotland*, Edinburgh: Scottish Government

Scottish Government (2011) *Gender-Based Violence Employee PIN (Partnership Information Network) Policy*, Edinburgh: Scottish Government

Scottish Government (2012a) *Integration and Inspiration: Final Report of the Gender-Based Violence and Health Programme in Scotland 2008–2011*, Edinburgh: Scottish Government

Scottish Government (2012b) *Chief Executive's Letter: Gender-Based Violence Action Plans*, Edinburgh: Scottish Government

Scottish Government (2012c) *A Guide to Getting It Right For Every Child*, Edinburgh: Scottish Government

Scottish Government (2014a) *Equally Safe: Scotland's Strategy for Preventing and Eradicating Violence Against Women and Girls*, Edinburgh: Scottish Government

Scottish Government (2014b) *Conduct of Relationships, Sexual Health and Parenthood Education in Schools*, Edinburgh: Scottish Government

Scottish Government (2015) 'Equally safe: Reforming the criminal law to address domestic abuse and sexual offences' (online). Available from URL: www.gov.scot/Resource/0047/00473932.pdf (accessed 2 November 2017)

Scottish Government (2016a) *Equally Safe: Scotland's Strategy for Preventing and Eradicating Violence Against Women and Girls – Update*, Edinburgh: Scottish Government

Scottish Government (2016b) *Health and Social Care Delivery Plan*, Edinburgh: Scottish Government

Scottish Government (2016c) *Supporting Children's Learning: Implementation of the Education (Additional Support for Learning) (Scotland) Act 2004*, Edinburgh: Scottish Government

Scottish Government (2016d) *Scottish Crime and Justice Survey 2014/15: Main Findings*, Edinburgh: Scottish Government

Scottish Government (2017a) *Criminal Proceedings in Scottish Courts 2015–2016* Edinburgh: Scottish Government. Available from URL: www.gov.scot/Resource/0051/00516039.pdf (accessed 2 November 2017)

Scottish Government (2017b) 'Scottish schools' (online). Available from URL: www.gov.scot/Topics/Education/Schools (accessed 24 November 2017)

Scottish Needs Assessment Programme (1997) *Domestic Violence,* Glasgow: Women's Health Network, NHS Scotland

Smaoun, S. (2000) *Violence Against Women in Urban Areas: An Analysis of the Problem from a Gender Perspective,* United Nations Urban Management Program, Working paper No. 17, Nairobi: UN Habitat

Social Work (Scotland) Act (1968) 'Chapter 49' (online). Available from URL: www.legislation.gov.uk/ukpga/1968/49/pdfs/ukpga_19680049_en.pdf (accessed 26 November 2017)

Stafford, A., Stead, J. and Grimes, M. (2007) *The Support Needs of Children and Young People Who Have to Move Home Because of Domestic Abuse,* Edinburgh: Scottish Women's Aid

Stanley, N. (2011), *Children Experiencing Domestic Violence: A Research Review,* Dartington: Research in Practice

Stanley, N., Ellis, J., Farrelly, N., Hollinghurst, S., Bailey, S. and Downe, S. (2015) 'Preventing domestic abuse for children and young people (PEACH): A mixed knowledge scoping review', *Public Health Research,* Vol. 3, No. 7; doi: 10.3310/phr03070

Stanley, N., Miller, P., Foster, H. R. and Thomson, G. (2011) 'A stop–start response: Social services' interventions with children and families notified following domestic violence incidents', *The British Journal of Social Work,* Vol. 41, No. 2, pp. 296–313

Stark, E. (2007) *Coercive Control: How Men Entrap Women in Personal Life,* Oxford: Oxford University Press

Stark, E. (2009) 'Rethinking coercive control', *Violence against Women,* Vol. 15, No. 12, pp. 1509–25

Stark, E. and Flitcraft, A. (1996) *Women at Risk,* London: Sage

Steel, N., Blakeborough, L. and Nicholas, S. (2011) *Supporting High-Risk Victims of Domestic Violence: A Review of Multi-Agency Risk Assessment Conferences (MARACs),* Research Report 55, London: Home Office

Stein, N. (1995) 'Sexual harassment in school: The public performance of gendered violence', *Harvard Educational Review,* Vol. 65, No. 2, pp. 145–63

SWA (2014) *Scottish Women's Aid Annual Report 2013–2014,* Edinburgh: Scottish Women's Aid

SWA (2016a) 'Scottish Women's Aid Census Day survey' (online). Available at URL: www.womensaid.scot/wp-content/uploads/2017/09/CensusDayDec2016.pdf (accessed 25 November 2017)

SWA (2016b) 'Scottish Women's Aid survey of funding for Women's Aid services' (online). Available at URL: www.womensaid.org.uk/research-and-publications/annual-survey-2016 (accessed 25 November 2017)

Taket, A. (2004) *Tackling Domestic Violence: The Role of Health Professionals,* Home Office Development and Practice Report 32, London: Home Office Research, Development and Statistics Directorate

Taylor, J., Bradbury-Jones, C., Kroll, T. and Duncan, F. (2013) 'Health professionals' beliefs about domestic abuse and the issue of disclosure: A critical incident technique study', *Health and Social Care in the Community,* Vol. 21, No. 5, pp. 489–99

Telfer, C. (2011) 'Education: Closing the achievement gap', in McKendrick, J. H., Mooney, G., Dickie, J. and Kelly, P. (eds) (2011) *Poverty in Scotland 2011*, London: Child Poverty Action Group, pp. 173–8

Thiara, R. K. and Gill, A. K. (2012) *Domestic Violence, Child Contact and Post-Separation Violence: Issues for South Asian and African-Caribbean Women and Children: A Report of Findings*, London: National Society for the Prevention of Cruelty to Children

Thomson, L. (2014) 'Challenging abuse together', Ministerial address by Lesley Thomson QC, Solicitor General for Scotland, COPFS Conference on Domestic Abuse (May 2014)

Trevillion, K., Oram, S., Feder, G. and Howard, L. M. (2012) 'Experiences of domestic violence and mental disorders: A systematic review and meta-analysis', *PLoS One*, Vol. 7, No. 12, e51740

UDHR (1948) 'Universal Declaration of Human Rights' (online). Available from URL: www.ohchr.org/EN/UDHR/Documents/UDHR_Translations/eng.pdf (accessed 23 November 2017)

UK Government Women and Equalities Committee (2016) 'Sexual harassment and sexual violence in schools' (online). Available from URL: www.publications. parliament.uk/pa/cm201617/cmselect/cmwomeq/91/9102.htm (accessed 26 November 2017)

UNCRC (1989) 'Convention on the Rights of the Child' (online). Available from URL: www.ohchr.org/Documents/ProfessionalInterest/crc.pdf (23 November 2017)

UNDP (2016) *Human Development Report 2016: Human Development for Everyone*, New York: United Nations Development Programme

Vallely, C., Robinson, A. L., Burton, M. and Tregidga, J. (2005) *Evaluation of Domestic Violence Pilot Sites at Caerphilly (Gwent) and Croydon*, London: Crown Prosecution Service

Virkki, T. (2015) 'Social and health care professionals' views on responsible agency in the process of ending intimate partner violence', *Violence Against Women*, Vol. 21, No. 6, pp. 712–33

Walby, S. (2009) 'The cost of domestic violence: Up-date 2009' (online), Project of the UNESCO Chair in Gender Research, Lancaster University. Available from URL: www.lancs.ac.uk/fass/doc_library/sociology/Cost_of_domestic_violence_update.doc (accessed 23 November 2017)

Walby, S. and Allen, J. (2004) *Domestic Violence, Sexual Assault, and Stalking: Findings from the British Crime Survey*, Home Office Research Study 276, London: Home Office

Walby, S., Towers, J., Balderston, S., Corradi, C., Francis, B., Heiskanen, M., Helweg-Larsen, K., Mergaert, L., Olive, P., Palmer, E. and Stöckl, H. (2017) *The Concept and Measurement of Violence Against Women and Men*, Bristol: Policy Press

Wallace, H. (2008) *Family Violence: Legal, Medical and Social Perspectives*, Boston, MA: Pearson

Ward, T. (2002) 'Good lives and the rehabilitation of sexual offenders: Promises and problems', *Aggression and Violent Behavior*, Vol. 7, pp. 513–28

Ward, T., and Gannon, T. A. (2006) Rehabilitation, aetiology, and self-regulation:

The comprehensive good lives model of treatment for sexual offenders', *Aggression and Violent Behavior*, Vol. 11, pp. 77–94

Warshaw, C. (1996) 'Domestic violence: Changing theory, changing practice', *Journal of the American Medical Women's Association*, Vol. 51, No. 3, pp. 87–91

Waterhouse, L. and McGhee, J. (2015) 'Practitioner–mother relationships and the processes that bind them', *Child & Family Social Work*, Vol. 20, No. 2, pp. 244–51

Wathen, C. N. and MacMillan, H. L. (2003) 'Interventions for violence against women: Scientific review', *JAMA*, Vol. 289, No. 5, pp. 589–600

Westmarland, N. (2016) *Violence Against Women: Criminological Perspectives of Men's Violences*, London and New York: Routledge

Westmarland, N. and Kelly, L. (2013) 'Why extending measurements of "success" in domestic violence perpetrator programmes matters for social work', *British Journal of Social Work*, Vol. 43, No. 6, pp. 1092–110

Westmarland, N., Thorlby, K., Wistow, J. and Gadd, D. (2014) 'Domestic violence: Evidence review' (online), N8 Policing Research Partnership. Available from URL: www.escholar.manchester.ac.uk/api/datastream?publicationPid=uk-ac-man-scw:225711&datastreamId=FULL-TEXT.PDF (accessed 1 March 2018)

Whiting, N. (2007) *A Contradiction in Terms? A Gendered Analysis & Same Sex Domestic Abuse*, Edinburgh: Scottish Women's Aid

WHO (2005) *Multi Country Study on Women's Health and Domestic Violence Against Women, Initial Results on Prevalence, Health Outcomes and Women's Responses*, Geneva: World Health Organization

WHO (2006) *Defining Sexual Health: Report of a Technical Consultation on Sexual Health, 28–31 January 2002*, Geneva: World Health Organization

WHO (2013) *Responding to Intimate Partner Violence and Sexual Violence Against Women: WHO Clinical and Policy Guidelines*, Geneva: World Health Organization.

WHO (2016) *Intimate Partner and Sexual Violence Against Women*, Geneva: World Health Organization

Wilkinson, R. G., and Marmot, M. G. (2003) *Social Determinants of Health: The Solid Facts*, Copenhagen: Regional Office for Europe, World Health Organization

Williamson, E. (2000) *Domestic Violence and Health: The Response of the Medical Profession*, Bristol: Policy Press

Wolfe, D. A., Crooks, C. V., Lee, V., McIntyre-Smith, A. and Jaffe, P. G. (2003) 'The effects of children's exposure to domestic violence: A meta-analysis and critique', *Clinical Child and Family Psychology Review*, Vol. 6, No. 3, pp. 171–87

Yllö, K. E. and Bograd, M. E. (eds) (1988) *Feminist Perspectives on Wife Abuse*, National Conference for Family Violence Researchers, 2nd, 1984 at the University of New Hampshire, Thousand Islands, CA: Sage

Zero Tolerance and YWCA Scotland (2011) *Under Pressure: Youth Worker Responses to Gendered Abuse and Exploitation*, Edinburgh: Zero Tolerance and YWCA Scotland.

INDEX